# WORKPLACE HOSTILITY

## Myth and Reality

## Gerald W. Lewis, Ph.D.
## and
## Nancy C. Zare, D.S.W.

**WORKPLACE HOSTILITY: Myth and Reality**

1  2  3  4  5  6  7  8  9  0

Technical development by Cindy Long. Edited by Sherri W. Emmons and Ed Cilurso. Printed by Braun-Brumfield Inc., Ann Arbor, MI.

**A CIP catalog record for this book is available from the British Library.**

The paper in this publication meets the requirements of the ANSI Standard Z39.48-1984 (Permanence of Paper).

**Library of Congress Cataloging-in-Publication Data**

Available from the publisher.

ISBN: 1-56032-5356-X (cloth)
ISBN: 1-56032-5364-8 (paper)

| USA | Publishing Office: | ACCELERATED DEVELOPMENT<br>*A member of the Taylor & Francis Group*<br>325 Chestnut Street<br>Philadelphia, PA 19106<br>Tel: (215) 625-8900<br>Fax: (215) 625-2940 |
|---|---|---|
| | Distribution Center: | ACCELERATED DEVELOPMENT<br>A member of the Taylor & Francis Group<br>47 Runway Road, Suite G<br>Levittown, PA 19057-4700<br>Tel: (215) 269-0400<br>Fax: (215) 269-0363 |
| UK | | ACCELERATED DEVELOPMENT<br>*A member of the Taylor & Francis Group*<br>1 Gunpowder Square<br>London EC4A 3DE<br>Tel: +44 171 583 0490<br>Fax: +44 171 583 0581 |

# WORKPLACE HOSTILITY

# ACKNOWLEDGMENTS

We want to thank many people who have helped us with this project. Michael McCourt, of MGM Associates, Inc., generously provided chapter 11, "Incorporating Security Technology and Personal Safety." His experience as a police officer and a consultant is highly valued. Dr. Jim Muller has worked with Dr. Lewis for more than 20 years. His ongoing work developing an at-risk assessment is highly valued and will add a great tool for providing mental health services. Terri Sorensen, the office manager at COMPASS, has rendered invaluable service and support on this project. In addition, she has maintained organization in an environment that often is frenzied.

We also want to thank all the people we have met at our training workshops and through our consultations. We have gained greatly from those experiences and have attempted to incorporate much of that knowledge in this project.

# Table of Contents

# List of Tables and Figures

# INTRODUCTION

When a troubled employee becomes violent at work, the event often receives major media coverage. We hear a steady stream of reports from a variety of sources citing numbers and statistics that increase our alarm, anxiety, and apprehension. In the last decade, the National Institute of Occupational Safety and Health (NIOSH) and the Centers for Disease Control (CDC) have become involved with issues of workplace violence and occupational homicide. NIOSH has become the primary source of information and statistics on workplace violence. Listed below are some facts and figures from reports generated by that agency:

- Between 1980 and 1989, there were 7,581 work-related homicides reported in the U.S. These represent 12% of all workplace fatalities. Homicide is now the third leading cause of death in the workplace.

- Homicide is the leading cause of death in the workplace for females. Yet male workers are three times more likely to be murdered at work than their female counterpart.

- Each week, an average of 20 people are murdered and 18,000 are assaulted while working or on-duty; this translates to 1,000 homicides and over 1 million assaults each year in the workplace.

- One in six deaths in the workplace is the result of violence.

- The rate of work-related homicide has tripled in the last 15 years.

Statistically, workplace violence differs significantly from homicide in the general population. According to NIOSH reports (1996b), in 1993 75% of work homicides were robbery-related, while only 9% of homicides in the general population involved robbery. In the same year, 47% of all murder victims knew their assailants, whereas the majority of work-related homicides were committed by strangers. Only 17% of female victims of workplace homicide were killed by a spouse or former spouse, but 29% of female victims in the general population were killed by "significant others." These reports indicate that workplace hostility and violence reflect different dynamics than those in the general population. Further, as we gain a greater understanding of these dynamics, we can develop better intervention strategies.

## PUTTING WORKPLACE VIOLENCE INTO PERSPECTIVE

While the statistics cited above are significant, noteworthy, and of serious import, we must view them in an objective and professional manner and not get carried away by the anxiety and apprehension that is sweeping our society. We must look at the numbers in a context that provides a more comprehensive view of workplace hostility. Bureau of Labor Statistics data from 1992 to 1994 indicate that 73% to 82% of all workplace homicides were committed during robberies; only 9% to 10% were attributed to business disputes. Further, only 4% to 6% were committed by coworkers or former employees. Yet the current concern with "disgruntled workers" has reached mythic proportions, as reported in the *Current Intelligence Bulletin* (NIOSH, 1996a, June):

> The circumstances of workplace homicides differ substantially from those portrayed by the media and from homicides in the general population. For the most part, workplace homicides are not the result of disgruntled workers who take out their frustrations on coworkers or supervisors, or intimate partners and other relatives who kill loved ones in the course of a dispute; rather, they are mostly robbery-related crimes.

Considering that more than 120 million people are employed in this country, 1,000 deaths per year remains a very small percentage. Further, we must remember that violence is increasing in many places in our society—in the streets, in our schools, and in the home—not simply in our workplaces.

If we take the average of 1,000 workplace homicides a year and compare it to other statistics, we can see the realistic significance of the numbers.

In its *1994 Motor Vehicle Crash Data Report*, the Department of Transportation (DOT) reported that, in 1993, there were 40,150 road-related deaths in the U.S. Of these, 17,473 involved alcohol.

In its annual survey, the Bureau of Justice Statistics (1996) estimates the numbers of rapes, robberies, assaults, larcenies, burglaries, and motor vehicle thefts each year in the U.S. The 1996 survey reported 9.1 million instances of violence or personal theft and 27 million household crimes.

The FBI's *Uniform Crime Report: Crime in the U.S.*(FBI, 1995) reported that, from 1980 to 1994, nearly 13,600 American children under the age of 12 were killed as a result of nonnegligent murder or manslaughter. This averages to more than 950 per year. Of these children, 54% were victims of domestic or family violence, 80% knew or were acquainted with the killer, and 3% were killed by a baby-sitter. Only 6% of these homicides were committed by a stranger.

According to the CDC (FBI, 1995), between 10 and 15 children are killed each week by handguns, many at the hands of other children.

The point of reviewing these statistics is to remind ourselves that we live in a violent, crime-ridden society. Violence permeates all areas of our lives, including the workplace. As crime increases in the U.S.—due to a wide variety of sociological, psychological, economic, and cultural factors—the workplace remains a microcosm of the larger society, influenced by the similar factors.

We must remember that the majority of workplace homicides are committed as part of criminal activities, such as robberies. It is essential that we do not overreact to violence in the workplace and so create even greater anxiety and apprehension.

Certainly we cannot simply ignore hostility and violence in the workplace; however, we must address these problems with a sense of competence and consistency, not anxiety and apprehension. It might help to remember this: According to the NIOSH data (1996b), the percentage of workplace homicides remained about the same from 1980 to 1992, averaging .7 per 100,000 workers. *In fact, there were fewer workplace homicides in 1992 than in 1980-1982.*

As human resources, employee assistance, mental health, safety, and legal personnel continue to face transitions and turmoil in the workplace, the issue of workplace hostility and violence has become a major focus. While there are no guarantees in life, organizations can take measures to minimize their own and their employees' risk and exposure to both internal and external hostility. The goal of this book is to provide guidance, direction, and strategies for developing a comprehensive approach to managing hostility in the workplace.

# Chapter 1

# A BRIEF HISTORY OF SAFETY IN THE WORKPLACE

As we move toward the 21st century, there is an increasing effort to improve the physical and emotional health of the workplace. In order to appreciate these efforts, it may be helpful to compare the workplace of today to that of 100 to 150 years ago. During the 1800s, the workplace was involved primarily in manufacturing, and the goal was to improve production through industrial technology. Businesses tried develop faster methods of production at lower costs. The factory setting saw the increase of mass-produced items through assembly lines and cookie-cutter technology. Most of the labor force was male, unskilled, with little education. Minimal concern was demonstrated for the welfare of the American worker.

It wasn't until the mid 1800s that child labor laws began to appear. Other than that, the primary effort in U.S. industry was to deliver as much product as possible for the lowest cost, regardless of the physical or emotional impact on workers. It was commonplace for workers to be at the workplace 12 to 16 hours a day, six days a week. Working conditions often were close to intolerable, with limited light and ventilation. Safety was of little concern, and workers were subject to illness and injury on a regular basis. If a worker was injured or became ill, he was removed—with no benefits or compensation. Minimum wage standards were nonexistent, and many workers toiled under some form of indentured arrangement for subsistence survival. The benefits we take for granted—overtime, vacations, sick leave, federal and religious holidays, personal days, family leave, health and disability insurance, retirement plans, worker's compensation, unemployment insurance, tuition reimbursement, COBRAs, and outplacement services—did not exist in the 1800s, even in the minds of the most forward-thinking employers.

It does not take much effort to imagine the workplace of yesteryear. Typically it was an evil-smelling, dirty, hazardous environment in which children and adults worked side by side, confronting the possibility of disabling injury and illness each day. In many cases, workers eked out their survival in factories, on farms, in mines, or in street markets fraught with violence and hostility that, in all likelihood, make our concerns of today pale by comparison.

The labor movement of the early 1900s did a great deal to change the look of the U.S. workplace. Child labor laws were written and enforced, and minimum wage standards and reasonable work hours became the focus of the labor movement. Eventually, employers—under pressure from labor unions to take better care of their employees—began to offer "benefits" to their workers. The majority of these benefits coincided with the initiation of the Social Security system and the return of young soldiers from World War II. The last 50 years have seen a dramatic improvement of conditions in the American workplace.

As the country moved into the postwar years, a shift began in the U.S. economy—a shift from manufacturing to service and information. Office buildings, shopping malls, and industrial parks began replacing factories, farms, and family businesses as primary employers.

In addition—and equally important—the emerging influence of psychology in the United States extended to the workplace, and its impact was felt on a number of levels. One significant concept that emerged from the marriage of industrial and behavioral psychology was that of *individual reward and incentive*. Citing studies of pigeons and laboratory rats, psychologists demonstrated to employers that the productivity of their workers could be increased through a system of planned rewards and incentives. This era saw the advent of incentive plans and improved working conditions. Commission-based salaries, bonuses, gifts, employee-of-the-month awards, favored parking places, promotions, and comp time were tied to employee performance in an ongoing effort to improve productivity.

Psychology departments at universities across the country received grants to conduct studies of the workplace: They were asked to determine what environments were most conducive to employee productivity, what schedules coincided with high-energy levels, even what colors helped workers feel more comfortable. By the 1970s, comfort was the operative word in most offices, as climate control, sound control, lighting, carpeting, artwork, and music were integrated into the workplace. By the 1990s, *ergonomics* (the applied science of equipment design, intended to maximize productivity by reducing operator fatigue and discomfort) emerged as a new field. It was no longer enough to make the environment look, sound, and smell good; in order for the individual worker to achieve his or her greatest potential (productivity), the employer had to provide equipment that assured the worker's optimum level of physical comfort.

In 1970, the Environmental Protection Agency (EPA) took on the issue of environmental safety and wielded great power to influence the workplace with respect to safe disposal of harmful byproducts. In 1972, the Occupational Safety and Health Administration (OSHA) was established to ensure that U.S. workplaces maintained safety standards for employees. Time and money were spent on safety committees, educational programs, and management training, as physical safety became an all-important focus of the workplace.

Coincident with these changes in the physical environment at work was a growing commitment to making the emotional atmosphere safe and comfortable. As the waves of the civil rights movement washed across the country during the 1960s, the ripples certainly were felt in the workplace. Antidiscrimination policies, quotas, and affirmative action became common in the workplace. As women entered the workforce in greater numbers, policies against gender discrimination and harassment proliferated. Former bastions of male domination—such as fire protection, law enforcement, medicine, and the military—were forced to change in order to accommodate the influx of female applicants. At the same time, federal and state legislatures enacted laws dealing with age discrimination, sexual orientation, and workers with disabilities. In the past 50 years we have seen dramatic efforts to improve the physical safety, personal comfort, and emotional welfare of workers. The workplace of today is safer, more comfortable, and less hostile than at any time in recorded history.

However, we must continue our efforts in this country to increase safety and security in the workplace. The worker of today is under a different type of stress in a different type of work environment than in the past. Estimates are that today's worker is doing one-third more work than he or she was a decade ago. Changes in technology, downsizing, mergers, layoffs, reorganizations, and the ever-present possibility of relocation put today's workers in a near-constant state of apprehension and anxiety.

It is relationships in the workplace that lubricate the pistons of production. Without adequate interpersonal relations, a workplace may grind to a halt like a car with an oil leak. The transitions in the workplace over the last decade have caused a dramatic erosion in these relationships. The interpersonal comfort that enabled teams of personnel to produce at a high level of efficiency has been diminished. Old colleagues have been replaced with new employees or with temps, per diem workers, consultants, independent contractors, or other contingent employees. New department heads with no relationship to workers have been brought in to clean house, reorganize, or facilitate transitions.

Take the case of an advertising company that was in the process of transition. Each employee, including the CEO, had been with the company for more than a dozen years, and they had developed an effective team that produced top-quality work. The down side was that this highly paid team was aging, continuing to turn out the same kinds of advertising campaigns, showing little diversity and no response to changes in technology.

The company grew, but after two failed attempts to "go public," the board of directors made several significant changes within three months: First, they bought a small but highly advanced company that provided new technologies. Second, they removed the CEO and replaced him with a financial wizard, one who had helped other companies go public and then left after one or two years. The new CEO immediately laid off 20% of the staff and began using contract and freelance professionals who were hired on a project-by-project basis. Departments were shrunk, merged, disbanded, or relocated, and the benefit package was changed.

These efforts succeeded in getting the company the financial backing to go public. However, the damage to the interpersonal infrastructure was overwhelming and resulted in turmoil and tension. Workers felt resentment, guilt, abandonment, and anger.

In his books *Healing the Wounds* and *Breaking Free*, David Noer noted that these are common reactions to such dramatic transitions. Sometimes, these reactions are so intense that employees begin to act out their feelings toward the organization. This behavior may take the form of organized slow-downs, sick outs, and strikes. Or it may be expressed in increased absenteeism and decreased levels of productivity. Underlying chronic tension and conflicts that have lain dormant for years may erupt with surprising fury in acts of extreme hostility and even violence against persons or property.

## DEFINING HOSTILITY AND VIOLENCE

Hostility and violence can take many forms in the workplace, from sabotage and vandalism to rape and murder. Hostile and violent acts include any of the following:

- acts of racial, sexual, or age discrimination and harassment;

- tampering with data systems;

- vandalizing company property;

- threatening coworkers or a supervisor with assault;

- sending threatening letters, faxes, or voice mail messages;

- stalking coworkers or a supervisor;

- destroying another person's property (e.g., slashing tires);

- assaulting coworkers or a supervisor;

- killing coworkers or a supervisor; or

- committing suicide on or near a company facility.

Because the definition of hostile and violent acts has changed in the last decade, record-keeping has been inconsistent and incomplete. Using the guidelines above, we can cite some recent figures, but inconsistencies remain, as these figures demonstrate.

- Between 1980 and 1989, 111,000 incidents of hostile and violent acts in the workplace were reported.

- In the same time period, 7,581 work-related homicides were reported.

- One of every six deaths in the workplace is the result of violence.

- Each year in the U.S., 1,000 homicides are committed at work.

- Homicide accounts for 12% of job-related deaths.

## Workplace Violence

One of the problems with any discussion of workplace violence is that the terminology is unclear and poorly defined. The Nova Scotia Occupational Health and Safety Advisory Council set up a working group to define workplace violence. In March 1995, the group arrived at a definition that included *nonphysical* as well as *physical* forms of behavior.

> Workplace violence means the attempted, threatened, or actual conduct of a person that endangers or is likely to endanger the health and safety of a worker, including any threatening statement, harassment, or behavior that gives a worker reasonable cause to believe that the worker's health and safety is at risk.

## Workplace Harassment

The work group went on to define harassment as

> any objectionable conduct, comment or display by a person that: 1) is directed at a worker; 2) endangers the health or safety of the worker; and 3) is made on the basis of race, creed, religion, color, sex, sexual orientation, marital status, family status, disability, physical size or weight, age, nationality, ancestry or place of origin.

This definition leads to some important questions: Is verbal harassment truly as damaging as a fist fight, rape, or murder? Is there a difference between verbal and physical gay bashing? How is it defined if two male workers get into a fight over a female employee? What about a fight over one employee getting a promotion over another?

Even in the case of murder, the legal system recognizes different factors involved in determining the degree of homicide. Issues such as intent, premeditation, diminished capacity, negligence, and self-defense are components of defining the type of homicide. Likewise, courts take into account several factors in categorizing an act as assault, aggravated assault, self-defense, assault with a deadly weapon, assault with intent to kill, and so on. With respect to violence in the workplace, the same qualifying definitions must be applied; otherwise, the entire discussion becomes muddled and confused. So, for the purpose of this discussion, we differentiate between acts that are a nuisance, a conflict, hostile, or violent (see Table 1.1).

A *nuisance act* may be annoying and offensive to others, but it does not have any direct malicious intent to a specific individual or group. Examples of nuisance acts might be offensive gestures, swearing, off-color jokes, and graffiti. This behavior may be bothersome and disgusting, but it is more a function of immaturity or poor socialization than of violence.

*Conflict* refers to the normal disagreements that take place in all interpersonal relationships. Conflict is one of the necessary evils of human involvement. Whether personal, political, or professional in nature, conflicts do not damage the integrity of the relationship. In fact, conflict may lead to greater understanding and more intimacy in a relationship.

*Hostile acts* are those that are *nonphysical* but are certainly directed at a specific individual or group with the intent of inflicting some type of emotional harm. Examples of this are harassment and discrimination. Harassment usually is an *active* manifestation of an underlying negative attitude toward an individual or group. It is personal and targeted in an attempt to exert power through intimidation and manipulation. Harassment can come in the form of comments, threats, or acts of intimidation, regardless of their source (sexual, racial, personal).

*Violent behavior* involves the display of physical force against a person or property that results in personal injury or de-

**TABLE 1.1**
**Examples of Nuisance, Conflict, Hostility and Violence**

| Nuisance | Conflict | Hostility | Violence |
|---|---|---|---|
| offensive jokes, graffiti, off-color language, gestures | normal personal or professional disagreements that do not harm the integrity of the relationship | harassment and discrimination; verbal, physical, and written threats; stalking | physical contact with the intent to do harm to a person or property |

struction of property. All acts of hostility feel like violations to some degree. Neither hostility nor violence should be tolerated in the workplace. However, there must be a delineation between the two, rather than lumping all acts into the same category. Similarly, the discipline involved must be different, depending on the nature of the act.

The examples that follow demonstrate the need for viewing different incidents as distinct.

**Example 1.**   A young male employee comes to work with a litany of ethnic and sexual jokes. He presents these in a loud and offensive style, complete with bodily gestures and imitations of racial and sexual stereotypes. He is prodded along by the others, who laugh and applaud his "comic" presentation.

**Example 2.**   Two men in the workplace argue over their mutual interest in the same woman. As their competition escalates, so does their verbal exchange; a physical fight ensues. Although one of the men is clearly the provocateur, the other grabs a metal bar and hits the first, knocking him unconscious. The injured man receives medical attention at the workplace and is taken to the hospital by ambulance, where he remains for two days with a concussion and possible brain injury. The "violent" worker is immediately suspended from his job and faces possible termination. Later that night, he is arrested for assault and battery with a deadly weapon. He probably will face a civil lawsuit as well.

**Example 3.** A male employee repeatedly makes lewd gestures at a female employee. He often comments on her figure, touches himself sexually, and boasts about how he could satisfy her sexually if only she would let him. When rebuffed, he begins making comments about her sexual frigidity and talking about her to other men. At no time does he touch her, stalk her, or threaten her with any physical intent. Certainly he is a nuisance, and his behavior is inappropriate and harassing. However, at no time does he pose a threat of physical danger to the woman. In fact, the woman is taller and outweighs him by a good 10 pounds. Rightfully, the female employee initiates a sexual harassment complaint against him. He is disciplined at work, and there is some discussion about a civil suit should his behavior continue.

The differences between these incidents are obvious: They are examples of nuisance, violence, and hostility, respectively. Each suggests different intent and motivation, leading to different types of harmful behavior. Each requires different responses in the workplace and intervention by outside sources. To treat them all the same denies the credibility and seriousness of each situation.

## THE COST OF VIOLENCE AND HOSTILITY IN THE WORKPLACE

In 1994, the FBI's *Uniform Crime Report: Crime in the U.S.* (1995) indicated that about 1 million individuals fall victim to some form of violence in the workplace each year. This represents about 15% of all violent crimes committed annually in this country. The FBI report goes on to describe some significant findings:

- Sixty percent were categorized as "simple assaults."

- Eighty percent were committed by males.

- In 84% of the incidents, there were no reported injuries.

The FBI report also indicated that violent crime in the workplace causes half a million employees to miss approximately 1.75

million days of work annually, or an average of 3.5 days per incident, resulting in approximately $55 million in lost wages.

NIOSH data varied slightly, indicating that 1 million American workers reported being physically assaulted at work, resulting in 876,000 lost work days and $16 million in lost wages. For 1992, NIOSH (1996b) reported that the medical costs of these assaults topped $13 billion.

In 1993, a joint study undertaken by the National Safe Workplace Institute and Behavior Analysts and Consultants, Inc., estimated that American companies spent more than $4 billion coping with the impact of workplace violence (Kenney, 1995). The study also reported that medical costs from workplace violence topped $13.5 billion in 1992, and $15 billion in 1993.

Another study by Bates and Donnell (1993) reported that juries awarded an average of $2.2 million for a workplace-related deaths and $1.8 million for workplace rapes.

Courts view the workplace as fertile ground for liability cases, holding the employer and management personnel responsible for unsafe acts and behavior in the workplace. In March 1994, *Management Review* reported:

> Courts have ruled that employers owe a duty of care toward their employees, customers, and business associates to take reasonable steps to prevent violence on their premises and by their employees. Employers who ignore potential workplace violence may well find themselves involved in negligence suits for failing to provide a reasonably safe workplace or for hiring and supervising an employee who turns violent.

In the past decade, liability for wrongful death in the workplace has been well established. Ignoring the issue of workplace hostility no longer is tolerated and may prove to be costly. Clearly, hostility and violence are very costly to both the American workplace and the American worker. Dollars and cents do not reflect the emotional toll violence takes on the worker, coworkers, family members, and the community.

# Chapter 2

# PROFILE OF AN
# AT-RISK EMPLOYEE

Although the majority of workplace violence is not committed by workers themselves, the focus today is on the disgruntled worker and how to recognize and manage him or her. Since only 4% to 6% of violent workplace incidents occur between coworkers, this concern seems somewhat unwarranted and inappropriately directed. Nonetheless, in this chapter we will address this aspect of the workplace violence scenario.

Psychologists and sociologists have made great efforts to better understand the root causes of violence in our society. Ultimately, their goal is to determine who might become violent or hostile and to prevent the advent of such behavior. Psychologists, psychiatrists, and social workers have developed tests, performed forensic evaluations, and studied family backgrounds. Educators and sociologists have studied the impact of poverty, ethnicity, and culture. The government has instituted programs and policies, and built more prisons. Vast quantities of time and money have been spent trying to limit the degree of violence in our society.

Most of the information we have comes from retrospective analyses—that is, reviews of the data on individuals who have already committed violent acts. While this information is relevant and may be helpful in understanding violent individuals, it is of limited value as a predictive tool. During a training program conducted by Dr. Gerald Lewis, participants spent some time discussing and reviewing characteristics of the violent individual. One of the attendees (who happened to be a police officer) exclaimed, "You've just described half the guys in my department!" The point is that such characteristics may be overly inclusive. One person might possess many of the characteristics and never become violent, while another possesses only a few and commits violent acts. The news media is filled with stories of people who appeared quiet, respectful, and upstanding—good neighbors who seemed to show no potential for violence—who proceeded to kill their families or coworkers with little provocation.

A prime example is John Taylor, who worked for the Glen Falls post office in Orange, California, for 27 years. Mr. Taylor had received many performance commendations and was well-liked by his coworkers. On August 10, 1989, he reported to work, shot two colleagues, then roamed the building dispensing 20 rounds before shooting himself in the head. It was later discovered that he had killed his wife before leaving for work that morning. Neighbors and friends reported that the couple had seemed happy and close, and that there were no indications of marital duress. Although, in hindsight, there may have been warning signs, by all reports Mr. Taylor evidenced none of the known warning signs of potential violence.

While hostile or violent acts can be committed by anyone (as demonstrated by Mr. Taylor), many violent individuals do share certain characteristics. Often, an individual who commits violence has already come to the attention of management because of difficulties in the workplace. Typically, the person is described as "disgruntled" by coworkers, supervisors, and friends. Although the individual may keep a low profile prior to the incident, he or she usually provides hints of an impending crisis. Events may escalate if early cues are not identified and defused. The hostile or violent act seldom is an isolated event but, rather, the end point along a continuum of reactions to increasing stress. The individual who becomes violent often feels inadequate, ashamed, and out of control, and views the violent act as a solution to the imbalance. The goal for employers is to become proficient at recognizing signposts along the path, and then to respond in a timely manner.

## CHARACTERISTICS OF VIOLENT EMPLOYEES

Figure 2.1 lists some common characteristics of individuals who have responded violently in the workplace. Knowing these characteristics may help in determining who is at risk for violent behavior.

- Is male, between the ages of 30 and 50

- Abuses alcohol or drugs

- Has a past history of violent behavior

- Has a past history of serious psychiatric disorder

- Has a past history of impulsive behavior

- Is familiar with and owns weapons

- Has exhibited compulsive behavior

- Has a history of trauma, abuse, or neglect

- Uses denial and projection

- Is isolated or a loner, with limited social outlets

- Has a strong identity with his or her job

- Has had frequent job transitions or enmeshment

- Has feelings of shame or humiliation

**Figure 2.1.** Common characteristics of individuals who have responded violently in the workplace.

## Male, Between the Ages of 30 and 50

It is not news that men tend to be more violent than women. Study after study bears this out. Researchers continue to question whether this is due to biological, sociological, or cultural factors. At this point, the nature vs. nurture question is a moot one. By a ratio of 10 to 1, men commit the violent acts in most societies, whether against other men, women, or children, in the home, on the streets, or in the workplace.

In the United States, one may speculate that the age range of 35 to 50 reflects the largest cohort within the workplace: the baby boom generation. But there are many factors that contribute to men in this age range being the most prone to workplace violence:

- Many men in this cohort are war veterans.

- Typically it is when they are in their mid-30s or 40s that people experience marital transitions.

- Mid-life is a time of increased angst, as we "lose" our children to adolescence and, perhaps, one or both of our own parents to death.

- This is the time when dreams of greater status and wealth meet with the reality of economics and downsizing. This collision may bring a meaningful loss of self-worth to an individual who already has an impaired level of self-esteem.

- The loss of a significant relationship, the disruption of parental roles, and financial disorganization may all be cumulative factors, as well.

## Alcohol and/or Substance Abuse

Alcohol and substance abuse are clear indicators of impaired judgment. Although our society has developed a growing awareness of the effects of drugs and alcohol, and is now into a second decade of education on the subject, substance abuse clearly remains a major sociological problem. There is little question that drugs and violence are intimately related. As Gilligan (1996, p. 219) reported:

> Alcohol use has repeatedly been found to be correlated with violent behavior; for example, more than 50% of perpetrators or victims of murder and other serious violence have alcohol in their bloodstream at the time; diagnosed alcoholics commit crimes at a much higher rate than do their nonalcoholic peers; a large percentage of violent criminals are alcoholics.

Whether a person is dealing on the street or using in the home or workplace, drug abuse often is a precursor to violence. And although alcohol is a legal drug, and so may not be subject to the same street influences, it also contributes to impaired judgment, loss of inhibitions, and diminished self-control.

Individuals in the workplace who act out with hostility or violence often have alcohol or substance abuse problems. Frequently, these problems are known to many colleagues, but little is done to intervene—not because of fear or lack of concern, but because of limited understanding, knowledge, or resources. The manager of today is under such pressure to get the work out with a downsized department, he or she has very little time to worry about the welfare of workers. Further, many managers receive little or no training on how to recognize troubled employees and what to do with them. Most organizations also do not have employee assistance programs. Many workplaces today are suffused with a great sense of demoralization—a state often denied by upper management focused on corporate survival.

No one factor or person is to blame for this scenario, yet it is at the core of many problems in today's workplace. The impaired employee may slip through the disciplinary cracks as a result of corporate denial, discomfort, or disorganization. Often we hear, "Oh, Harry ... well he's a drunk, but he's been working here for years. No one does anything about it." Or, "Sue, she gets away with murder. She's always calling in sick, but we know she was on a bender this weekend." Not addressing the situation only allows the problem to worsen. These impaired individuals may stabilize at a level of diminished capacity and be tolerated in the department, or they may continue along the course of their disease until they reach a crisis—violent or otherwise.

The cost to the rest of the department is high, as well. For workers trying to maintain a level of motivation, such problem colleagues are major sources of energy drain and emotional demoralization. The employee who works hard every day, then gets frustrated and "shoots his mouth off" at management, receives a disciplinary action. But the impaired employee often is tolerated for months and even years without consequences. To many workers, it seems unfair and inconsistent.

An employee with a drug or alcohol problem is a danger in the workplace and at much greater risk for hostility and violence. Alcohol and drug abuse contributes to job performance impairment across the board, and should not be ignored in any case.

## History of Violent Behavior

Research indicates that many individuals who commit violent acts demonstrate an escalation of behavior prior to the episode. In today's harried workplace, hiring practices often are lax, and people with criminal records for violent behavior are hired. This fact often comes to light only after the individual becomes violent again. But the individual often displays an increase in inappropriate behavior (on or off the job) that only gradually escalates to a violent episode. Often these signal behaviors go by without a response. Listed below are some examples of such behaviors:

- frequent arguments with coworkers or supervisors that become abusive and include loud and foul language;

- fights at home when the person has left his or her family or a restraining order has been implemented;

- trouble with the police for disorderly conduct;

- inappropriate behavior at parties, bars, social gatherings.

Often, the troubled behavior is common knowledge at the workplace but management does nothing, because the problems are seen as happening outside of work. Although this may be the case, and it may be inappropriate for a supervisor to address the issue, the behavior should be noted as an indicator of potential risk.

## History of a Serious Psychiatric Disorder

Many believe that "crazy" people are the ones who commit violent crimes. TV has played up the image of the deranged person who hears voices commanding him or her to go out and murder others. There are, in fact, real-life cases of such individuals, and the media capitalizes on their stories. People remember the "Son of Sam" serial killer, who terrorized New York several years ago; John Chapman, who killed John Lennon after "receiving messages" from *The Catcher in the Rye*; and, more recently, Andrew Cunanen, who went on a murder/suicide spree that included Gianni Versace.

**Character Disorders.** Statistics show that people with psychotic diagnoses—such as paranoid schizophrenia, schizoaffective disorder, and manic-depressive disorder—do not often respond with violence. Rather, as Gilligan (1996) reported, it is individuals with *character disorders* who tend to strike out against others when they experience a narcissistic injury. People with character disorders may appear to be "normal," but have occasional personality "quirks." This is the person others describe this way:

He has a quick temper.

He can't take a joke.

She can't let things go.

He tries to be a big shot.

He always has to be right.

She has no conscience.

He believes his own lies.

She can cheat and justify it.

Such people often harbor extremely strong feelings toward other individuals or groups. People with character disorders have difficulty making attachments and developing a full sense of conscience.

**Mental Disorders.**   Although people with serious mental disorders do not usually respond with violence, they may react to stressful situations with a wide range of inappropriate behaviors. Most notably, disorders that involve paranoid ideations and persecutory delusions leave the individual vulnerable to misperceptions and misunderstandings of normal social interactions. People diagnosed with paranoid schizophrenia, paranoid personality, borderline personality disorder, manic-depression, and chronic depression are especially prone to these types of thought impairments.

In addition, suicidal ideation and activities often are symptoms of serious emotional conditions. Self-abuse or "soft" self-destructive behavior—misuse of medication, poor personal hygiene, risk-taking behavior, indiscriminate sexual behavior, gambling, drinking, and disregard for important duties and responsibilities (i.e., neglecting visits with children after a divorce or not making insurance payments)—also may be symptoms that need attention.

**Neurological Disorders.**   It also should be noted that neurological disorders may impact a person's cognitive processes, resulting in delusional thinking. Tumors, encephalitis, syphilis, Parkinson's disease, blood infections, and other central nervous system disorders may cause temporary or permanent distortions in brain processes. Often, mental health professionals overlook the biological etiology of distorted thought processes that could result in serious aggressive behavior.

**Erotomania.**   Another type of thought disorder often is described as *romantic obsession* or *erotomania*. This is an intense attachment to another person. Although it may at first appear to be romantic affection, it is a much deeper attachment that often reaches fanatic proportions. At times, the person who is the focus of the attachment is not even aware of it. Signs of this type of disorder may not be overt; they run the gamut from anonymous calls, notes, and letters to stalking, stealing personal objects, and maintaining a shrine to the focus individual. Such a shrine might include the stolen objects along with pictures, articles, poems, and drawings.

The person suffering erotomania often fantasizes about the object of affection, and may change his or her entire life in order to fulfill the attachment. When object of this attachment becomes aware of the malformed relationship, he or she usually rejects the pursuer. Often, this does little more than feed the fantasies and intensify the desire. The delusional person may incorporate the rebuff as "part of the plan," leading to a more malignant level of pursuit. When management at work or law enforcement agencies are brought into the picture and rejection finally becomes a reality for the person, it may lead to a crumbling of defenses and an acting out in the form of a homicide/suicide, leaving the final message: "If I can't have you, no one can."

It is important to note that, statistically, people with obvious mental illnesses are not the ones mostly likely to become violent, unless in an acute psychotic state in which they feel extreme threat. Rather, it often is the person with a character disorder—one who demonstrates less flagrant symptoms—who acts out in violence.

## History of Impulsive Behavior

In addition to a history of violent or self-destructive behavior, the violence-prone individual may demonstrate a pattern of impulsive behaviors like these:

- frequent job changes for little reason;

- a sudden interest or disinterest in hobbies and activities;

- frequent short-term social and romantic relationships characterized by intense beginnings and stormy endings;

- purchase of products beyond his or her capacity (cars, homes, TVs, motorcycles, clothing, etc.);

- involvement in poorly-thought-out investment plans; and

- moving from one geographic location to another for little apparent reason.

These kinds of activity may indicate a pattern of impulsiveness—behavior the person engages in without adequate thought or planning.

## Familiar With and Owns Weapons

The majority of workplace homicides involve firearms. While people seldom purchase weapons in order to complete a violent act, if weapons are easily available, an at-risk person might use them impulsively to "solve a problem."

Having said this, it is important to note that when an individual suddenly purchases a gun, seemingly on impulse, it should be viewed with some concern. A sudden gun purchase could be an indicator of potential problems, including the development of a paranoid ideation. In fact, from a prognostic and predictive perspective, the man whose father bought him his first gun when he was a teenager—one who has learned to use weapons properly and with respect—is less of a concern than the one who has never owned a weapon before and suddenly buys one on impulse.

Ownership of and familiarity with weapons often is touted as characteristic of potentially violent individuals. However, in and of itself, gun ownership is relatively meaningless unless viewed in a larger context.

## History of Compulsive Behavior

Compulsive behavior can take many forms, but most often it is evidenced in "bad habits" or addictions, such as drinking, abusing drugs, gambling, smoking, overeating, and sexual promiscuity. Compulsivity is the behavioral component to obsessive thinking, which may manifest itself in such behaviors as erotomania.

Much research has been devoted to the etiology of compulsive behaviors, since many of them are self-destructive if not socially impairing. The question of biological versus psychological origin often is raised in this research, since family history sometimes is associated with these behaviors. However, some psychologists theorize that compulsive behaviors often are manifested to defend an individual against emotional discomfort. Many people describe the compulsive behavior as "having a life of its own" or as a "monkey on my back." The individual often feels controlled by it, rather than the reverse. However, the activity itself often is soothing, albeit temporarily, and has a calming effect on the person. Often, the behavior escalates and becomes central to the individual's life, subsequently damaging him or her physically and emotionally and hurting his or her social relationships.

### History of Trauma, Abuse, or Neglect

People who commit hostile and violent acts often have a history of being the recipients of such treatment. It must be clarified that not all people who experience abuse or neglect as children grow up to be violent adults; however, those people who are violent often have very troubled pasts. Many were victims of childhood abuse and neglect. Being victimized is extremely damaging to self-esteem and self-image; such abuse plants the seeds for malformed emotional development.

In response to such abuse, people typically develop defense mechanisms that help to ward off intense feelings of humiliation, shame, loss of control, abandonment, "unlovability," rage, distrust, and dependency. These defense mechanisms often take the form of impulsiveness and compulsivity, alcohol or substance abuse, mood swings, intense relationships, or risk-taking behaviors. The person's ability to modulate emotional reactions and feelings becomes impaired; he or she often is seen as overreacting or underreacting to situations.

### Use of Denial and Projection

Underlying all defense mechanisms is the basic building block of denial. The goal of our emotional defenses is to protect us from painful experiences, past or present. So all defense mechanisms may be viewed as various forms of denial. In a psychotic person, the denial is so primitive and raw that the psychotic process blocks out reality, and the individual manufactures a new reality in which the pain is not experienced.

Others forms of denial may have their origins in biological or developmental processes. For example, as adults we cannot remember being born, being nursed, teething, or learning to walk. Most of us cannot remember learning to talk, toilet train, or many other experiences from our early years. We know these events did occur for each of us, yet they are not a part of our conscious experience. This may be considered as an example of repression and denial, whereby the event is not experienced on a conscious level.

Projection is a manifestation of the denial process whereby the individual takes feelings, thoughts, and reactions that are too painful to experience and projects them into the world and onto others. The classic example of this is the man who is fearful of underlying homosexual concerns, and so must block them from his consciousness. He then sees homosexuals as a personal threat to him and society. He may act on these projections—assuming a very macho style, womanizing, or even "gay bashing"—as a way of externalizing the internal conflict. Similarly, people who grew up in abusive and neglectful homes may see the world as a hostile and untrustworthy place; they may develop a personal motto of, "Do it to them, before they do it to you." In such a world view, no one is to be trusted; anyone doing something nice for you is seen as having an ulterior motive.

All people use varying degrees of denial and projection as part of their defense structures. As we grow older and develop, we find more highly organized and less primitive ways to implement these key ingredients of psychic protection.

For a model for psychological development, we can look at a computer and its programs. Before we can run a program, we must have the adequate hardware: a computer with enough memory, a printer, monitor, modem, and so on. In addition, we must have the proper training to install and run the program. If the hardware is insufficient or our training is inadequate, the computer cannot carry out its functions efficiently.

Similarly, the human being must be born with adequate hardware, in the form of a capable brain and physical body. Any brain impairment—such as mental retardation, fetal alcohol syndrome, or other neurological damage—affects the functioning of the hardware and, regardless of the software, the system may not run. Parents, family, friends, and teachers function as the programmers, inputting our data and programs. If our "programmers" are influenced by their own upbringing, drugs and alcohol, or cultural and religious orientations, our programming may reflect these limitations. So we may all experience difficulties performing some tasks due to hardware or software problems, be they physical, mental, or emotional.

To carry the analogy, a person may have adequate hardware and software; but somewhere along the line a "virus" is introduced, and the person experiences a shutdown, either temporary or permanent, in the form of a serious physical or emotional illness.

In all of these ways, an individual's psychic structure may develop with gaps, limitations, and inadequacies. As we grow and develop, our defense systems are constantly being modified. People with limited defense systems must rely on immature methods to cope with the stresses of life. Their denial and projection are stronger, and they tend to view the world in black and white, with a limited capacity to see moral shades of gray. They view others as either for them or against them. Things are either right or wrong, true or false. Thus, their ability to understand and empathize with others is impaired.

This primitive system of denial and projection is fertile ground for obsessive thinking, persecutory and paranoid ideation, and compulsive behaviors. As people face painful experiences with limited or damaged psychological armor, they may be unable to manage the subsequent emotional turmoil with an appropriate response.

### Isolated/Loner with Limited Social Outlets

Perhaps it is an obvious observation that individuals with the personality traits, emotional defenses, and behavioral characteristics discussed above may have difficulties with interpersonal relationships. They may be perceived by others as argumentative, noncompliant, and obstructionist. Often these folks are loners. They may be viewed as weird or different, and they tend to develop an isolated, uninvolved lifestyle that allows them to maintain a distance from others. This distant style may be covered with a hostile veneer that also serves to keep others at a distance.

## Strong Identity with Job

Given that at-risk individuals may have limited interpersonal skills, their lives may be underdeveloped and offer few social connections. One may speculate that friendships, marriages, parent-child relationships, and work relationships bear the brunt of impaired personality traits and behavioral manifestations. Therefore, the person's job takes on a significantly larger component in his or her identity. The person may have lost friends, family, money, and health, but he or she retains the role of employee, with its concomitant benefits of salary, pension, and personal prestige.

Today, both men and women identify with their job titles; traditionally, however, this has been a strong underlying component of the male personality. Career choice, social status, financial security, and the power gained from employment play a significant role in ego development for men. This identification with a job is a normal process for all people; however, some people over-identify with their jobs or develop enmeshed relationships with them to the point that they feel diminished without them. These individuals feel that their power, status, and very existence are connected to their careers, and the threat or reality of job-loss is overwhelming.

For the man who has nothing but his job, the loss looms as a crushing event. It is as if he says, "I've lost my wife and kids. I'm living in a tiny apartment. I don't have any friends, but I have my job. If I lose my job, I have nothing left." Changes at work, perceived or real threats to status, a new supervisor, new technology, layoffs, and disciplinary actions may be viewed from a position of denial and projection, resulting in suspicion and mistrust. The man experiences changes at work as *personal*, not *personnel*. He feels persecuted and victimized in the workplace, displaying an extreme manifestation as paranoid ideation.

## Frequent Job Transitions and Enmeshment

Although the science of human behavior has not developed to the point where we can predict whether any given individual will respond with hostility or violence, warning signs can help identify troubled employees. Troubled employees are those whose personal problems interfere with their ability to work to standard. Often, they have difficulty with authority figures or other employees.

In recent years, as companies have downsized in response to competition, the opportunity to leave one organization for another has diminished. Many workers find themselves not liking their jobs, their bosses, or their coworkers, but they feel trapped by their paychecks, benefits, and seniority. Often, such troubled employees develop a hostile-dependent relationship with the workplace, which leads to a variety of job performance impairments. The inability to leave the situation, along with the feeling of being trapped, may result in behaviors that become increasingly inappropriate and potentially at-risk.

Only a small percentage of troubled employees become at-risk employees who are prone to hostile or violent behavior.

## THE ROLE OF SHAME

In his book *Violence* (1996), James Gilligan posited that shame and humiliation are the leading causes behind individual and national violent behaviors.

> The emotion of shame is the primary or ultimate cause of violence whether toward others or toward self. The different forms of violence, whether toward individuals or entire populations, are motivated (caused) by the feeling of shame. The purpose of violence is to diminish the intensity of shame and to replace it as far as possible with its opposite, pride, thus preventing the individual from being overwhelmed by the

feeling of shame. It is important to add that men who feel ashamed are not likely to become seriously violent toward others and inflict lethal or life-threatening, mutilating or disabling injuries on others unless several preconditions are met (p. 110).

Gilligan went on to list these preconditions: The individual feels chronically and acutely ashamed as a result of lifelong experiences of humiliation and disparagement. This shame-based personality often is covered by a defensive mask of bravado, arrogance, machismo, or indifference.

These men perceive themselves as having no nonviolent means of warding off or diminishing their feelings of shame or low self-esteem.

The person lacks the emotional capacities that normally inhibit the violent impulses that are stimulated by shame. Most important are love and guilt toward others and fear for self. ... The person who is overwhelmed by feelings of shame is by definition experiencing a psychiatrically life-threatening lack of love, and someone in that condition has no love left for anyone else. ... A central precondition for committing violence, then, is the presence of overwhelming shame in the absence of feelings of either love or guilt (pp. 111–113).

The lack of fear seems to be concomitant with the lack of love and guilt. Often at-risk people willingly engage in behavior they know will result in their own deaths rather than experience further shame, degradation, and humiliation. They prefer death to dishonor or, more importantly, disrespect.

As we look for the warning signs of violence-prone individuals, we must be acutely aware of those who have shame-based personalities—most notably, paranoid personalities and those with antisocial or psychopathic/sociopathic disorders. When making an assessment, we must look for life experiences that sow the seeds of severe shame and humiliation. Examples of this are childhood experiences of physical and sexual abuse, severe neglect and abandonment, extreme rejection by peers, and chronic academic failure. In adolescence and adulthood, examples include social or sexual rejection, imprisonment, combat experience, and unsuccessful attempts at overachievement.

When doing an assessment, we must listen for the individual's experience of an incident, and not interpret the event through our own experiences. It is imperative to remember that it is not necessarily the event but *the individual's experience of the event* that triggers a violent outburst. As Gilligan noted, it often is a trivial event, filtered through layers of preexisting shame and degradation, that precipitates an extremely violent reaction.

# Chapter 3

# CONDUCTING
# AT-RISK ASSESSMENTS

As we noted earlier, it is difficult to accurately predict who will act out in a hostile or violent manner. Further, most violence in the workplace is not between coworkers, but is generated from outside the workplace (see chapter 4). However, there is growing concern over how to perform an evaluation on an individual who is showing signs of possible hostility or violence. Mental health professionals are being asked to do threat assessments, forensic evaluations, and fitness-for-duty evaluations—all of which we call *at-risk assessments*.

As more professionals are called upon to conduct assessments of employees who express some form of hostility, there is a growing need for a more in-depth and extensive evaluation. We believe these evaluations are different from the general clinical assessments that are performed on most individuals referred for mental health services. Many professionals are unwilling to provide such evaluations because they do not feel they have the skill or training needed. They are unwilling to make a determination of violence potential because it is so difficult to do so accurately. Nonetheless, these evaluations are necessary to maintain a safe and productive workplace.

Dr. Gerald W. Lewis and Dr. James Muller have developed an at-risk evaluation procedure that includes three factors:

1.  A comprehensive structured interview

2.  Consultation with management

3.  Psychological testing

## IMPROVING COMPLIANCE

Many people referred for at-risk evaluations feel persecuted and anxious about the procedure. In order to do a reliable assessment, you must enlist the person's compliance. There are several things you can do to improve the employee's attitude and compliance. By phone contact, letter, and in the initial interview, you should fully explain the process to the person, informing him or her of all discussions that have taken place, what the evaluation procedure involves, and who will receive a copy of the summary report. Offering him or her a copy of the report may reduce the anxiety and concern. Tell the employee that he or she may bring along a concerned party (a spouse, union representative, friend, etc.). However, dissuade these "guests" from being present in the actual evaluation.

Prior to the evaluation, you should meet with management and get a clear understanding of the behaviors that are causing concern. Then review these behaviors with the employee, keeping the discussion focused on job performance. Explain that the purpose of the evaluation is to return the individual to work as soon as possible, with recommendations that will help ensure that the problem does not recur. Naturally, a comprehensive release form is used for this type of service. Whenever possible, send it to the employee ahead of time along with a letter describing the evaluation process.

## CONSULTING WITH MANAGEMENT

Often, a manager is concerned over an employee's behavior or threats and is not sure how to respond. In an ideal situation, all employees in the workplace would be trained in dealing with workers who are manifesting symptoms of stress that could result in a violent episode (see chapters 7 and 8).

When an employee is referred for an evaluation, a management consultation intake worksheet should be completed (see Figure 3.1). This worksheet provides information on the organization as well as the individual being referred. It asks, questions like these:

What are the behaviors that are causing concern?

How long has it been going on?

What is this employee's history with the company?

These and many other questions will help you determine exactly what is being evaluated. In addition, you should gather information about stresses within the organization that may be causing an increase in "toxicity," such as reorganization, downsizing, labor/management disputes, other accidents or acts of violence, and changes in benefits. Only after this management intake form is completed should you see the individual for an evaluation. Often, this kind of intake shows that an evaluation is not necessary, after all. Perhaps the supervisory personnel simply needs to consult on how to better manage the individual.

When an individual is referred for assessment, a more in-depth, structured evaluation is required to determine the person's potential risk. Figure 3.2 is an at-risk assessment worksheet that may be helpful in evaluating an individual's potential for violence. Figure 3.3 is an abbreviated draft of a personal problems checklist developed by Drs. Lewis and Muller. This self-administered questionnaire is a brief information-gathering tool rather than a statistically derived psychological test and can highlight certain life experiences that will be discussed during the evaluation. It can be

**Figure 3.1.** Management consultation intake worksheet.

Name of Organization:_____ Date:_____

Name of contact:_____ Position:_____

Name of at-risk employee:_____

Position:_____ Years with company:_____

Specific description of at-risk behavior:

      verbal threats        gestures        physical altercation

      phone calls        threatening notes      stalking

      destruction of property

      other:_____

Prior work experience within the company:_____

_____

_____

Previous disciplinary actions:_____

_____

_____

Stresses within the organization

      reorganizations      downsizing      transfers

      L/M difficulties      decrease in benefits      other hostility

      accidents/trauma/deaths

      other:_____

Specific questions and concerns of management:_____

_____

_____

Recommendations:_____

_____

_____

completed in approximately 15 minutes and administered along with other psychological questionnaires.

The entire evaluation process—including the management intake, psychological testing, structured interview, and management follow-up consultation—takes four to six hours. Figure 3.4 is an outline of the evaluation process.

## USING PSYCHOLOGICAL TESTS

New psychological tests can greatly improve assessment of at-risk employees. These instruments are better suited to the workplace than the clinically derived questionnaires of the past. Some of the advantages they offer are listed here:

*Brevity:* They contain fewer items and take less time to administer.

*Credibility:* The items are less clinically focused and more understandable, relevant, and related to workplace issues.

*Speed:* Rapid scoring provides results in a timely manner.

*Normative comparisons:* Through the use of computer scoring, the individual's performance can be compared to a large database.

Batteries usually consist of several paper-and-pencil questionnaires. Except for some ability tests, they are untimed. Individual tests in a battery take from 10 to 60 minutes each, and a typical battery can be completed in one to two hours by adults with a sixth-grade education. Same-day or next-day scoring is a standard feature.

The first psychological tests were developed in clinical settings and to measure mental disorders. Their success in identify-

*(Text continues on page 51.)*

**Figure 3.2.** At-risk assessment worksheet.

---

**Name:** _____ **Age:** _____

**Race:**   Caucasian   Black   Hispanic   Asian

**Marital status:**   Single   Married   Separated   Divorced
Widowed   Remarried   Living together

**Spousal status** (age, work, health, etc.): _____

_____

_____

**Children:**_____ Age: ___ Sex: ___

_____   ___   ___

_____   ___   ___

_____   ___   ___

biological/step          in home/out of home

### EDUCATION HISTORY

What was the highest grade you completed? _____

Did you repeat any years? If so, why?_____

_____

If we reviewed your academic record, how would it look?_____

_____

What type of disciplinary problems would we find?_____

_____

**Figure 3.2.** Continued

Did you belong to clubs, teams or extracurricular activities?_____

_____

_____

### MILITARY HISTORY

Branch of service:_____

Volunteer or draft:_____

Dates and places of service:_____

_____

_____

Type of service:_____

_____

_____

Highest rank achieved:_____

Discharge status:_____

Disability status:_____

### WORK HISTORY

Look for gaps, sudden departures, etc. If resume is blocked out by years, be sure to inquire about months in order to check for gaps.

Company:_____

Dates of employment:_____

**Figure 3.2.** Continued

Position:_____

Reason for leaving:_____

_____

_____

### HIGH-RISK HOBBIES/INTERESTS/ACTIVITIES

Be sure to assess interest in and access to weapons, gambling, drinking, membership in clubs, magazine subscriptions, etc.

_____

_____

_____

_____

### LEGAL/CRIMINAL RECORD

If we search your criminal record, what problems will we find?_____

_____

_____

Has anyone ever had to call the police as a result of your behavior?_____

_____

Have you ever been arrested, even if it did not result in a charge?_____

_____

Were you ever adjudicated to the Department of Youth Services or Department of Social Service?_____

_____

**Figure 3.2.** Continued

## DRIVING RECORD

If we search your driving record, what will we find?_____

_____

Have you ever been stopped for driving under the influence?_____

_____

Have you earned any surcharge points on your automobile insurance?_____

_____

## PREVIOUS AGGRESSIVE BEHAVIOR

When was the last time you were in a physical altercation of any type that
involved hitting, pushing, or grabbing?*_____

_____

_____

## ASSESSMENT OF CHILDHOOD RISK FACTORS

As a child, describe your involvement with the following:

     fire setting _____

     _____

     rough play _____

     _____

_____

*Do not use the word "fight," as many men interpret that as hitting with fists.

**Figure 3.2.** Continued

experimenting with or hurting animals_____

_____

self-inflicted injuries _____

_____

### SOCIAL/SEXUAL ASSESSMENT

Describe your social life as a teenager._____

_____

_____

Did you belong to a clique, have a lot of friends, and go to parties?_____

_____

Did you prefer individual activities or to hangout by yourself?_____

_____

Please describe your dating experience._____

_____

_____

Did you have long relationships with girlfriends, casual dates, or limited
social experiences?_____

_____

Please describe how you learned about sex and your first sexual encounters.

_____

_____

**Figure 3.2.** Continued

---

### FINANCIAL HISTORY

Include credit card debt, own/rent residence, bankruptcy, cars, college, child support/alimony, liens, etc.

If we do a credit check, what will it turn up regarding your finances?_____

_____

_____

_____

### SOCIAL ACTIVITIES

How do you enjoy spending your free time?_____

_____

_____

_____

What club and religious, civic, or hobby organizations do you belong to?

_____

_____

_____

What do you like to do on vacations?_____

_____

_____

_____

**Figure 3.2.** Continued

---

### SELF-DESCRIPTION OF PERSONALITY

How would others who work with you describe your personality?_____

_____

_____

What would they see as your strengths?_____

_____

_____

What would they see as your weaknesses?_____

_____

_____

How would your family answer the same questions?_____

_____

_____

_____

_____

If you could change something about your personality, what would it be?

_____

_____

_____

_____

**Figure 3.2.** Continued

## DRUG AND ALCOHOL HISTORY

Beginning with high school, tell me about your drug and alcohol use up to the present. _____

_____

Have you ever been told by others that you drink too much? _____

Have you thought about cutting down on your drinking? _____

How many times have you been intoxicated in the past year? _____

**Depression and Suicide Assessment**

Be sure to include yourself as well as your family of origin. _____

_____

_____

**Psychiatric/Substance Abuse Treatment History**

_____

_____

_____

## PSYCHOSOCIAL HISTORY

**Parent status** (Living, deceased, marital histories, work histories, personality types, relationship toward client, etc.): _____

_____

_____

**Figure 3.2.** Continued

**Sibling status** (Position, relationships, marital histories, work histories, relationship toward client):_____

_____

_____

Drugs and alcohol involvement in nuclear and extended family through grandparents:_____

_____

_____

Family psychiatric history:_____

_____

_____

_____

**History of abuse/neglect/trauma/tragedy during childhood:** (Ask specifically if the individual was mistreated physically or sexually as a child. Assess experiences of neglect, separations from parents, and familial tragedies. Assess extent of illnesses, operations, accidents, disabilities, or physical limitations. As a child, was the individual a victim of extreme teasing or bullying by other children?)_____

_____

_____

_____

_____

_____

_____

**Figure 3.3.** Personal problems checklist.

---

**Note:** This figure does not include the complete checklist, but a representation of the types of items.

**Instructions:** The purpose of this questionnaire is to identify areas of personal difficulty that may be explored during your interview. While positive aspects will be considered elsewhere in your assessment, this deals primarily with potentially troublesome life experiences.

---

Under each numbered list, check *any and all items* that are true about you.

Do not stop after one check mark. Read every item, as *several may apply.*

### GROWTH AND DEVELOPMENT

**Growing up, I had ...**

| | | |
|---|---|---|
| T | F | a birth injury |
| T | F | a physical handicap |
| T | F | parents who separated or divorced |
| T | F | a parent with a mental breakdown |
| T | F | a parent with a serious illness or injury |
| T | F | a parent who died |
| T | F | a sibling who died or had a serious illness |
| T | F | a foster home |
| T | F | adoptive parents |
| T | F | a serious illness or accident |
| T | F | counseling for emotional problems |

**One or both of my parents ...**

| | | |
|---|---|---|
| T | F | drank too much |
| T | F | used drugs |
| T | F | argued or fought more than most parents |
| T | F | strictly punished any bad behavior |
| T | F | had quick tempers |

# Figure 3.3. Continued

| | | |
|---|---|---|
| T | F | had their noses into everything I did |
| T | F | criticized the smallest mistakes |
| T | F | made constant demands on me |
| T | F | had to have things done their way or not at all |
| T | F | acted in an extremely protective way toward me |
| T | F | needed a great deal of help and assistance to cope |
| T | F | were indifferent to my needs |
| T | F | meant well, tried to do the right thing, but often couldn't cope |
| T | F | weren't around when I needed them |

**As a child or adolescent, I ...**

| | | |
|---|---|---|
| T | F | was teased, picked on, or bullied by other kids |
| T | F | was beaten by my parents or other adult relatives |
| T | F | was sexually mistreated |
| T | F | felt deserted or seriously neglected by my primary caretaker |
| T | F | set a fire on at least one occasion |
| T | F | experimented on an animal |
| T | F | experimented on myself to see how much pain I could take |
| T | F | stole money |
| T | F | defaced or damaged someone's things as a joke |
| T | F | often stole small items from stores |
| T | F | was pressured into sexual activities by a group |

## EDUCATION AND LEARNING

**In school, I stood out from the others because I ...**

| | | |
|---|---|---|
| T | F | was often scolded by the teacher |
| T | F | got into fights |
| T | F | lost my temper |

# **Figure 3.3.** Continued

T  F  skipped classes or came late

T  F  was put in detention

T  F  was suspended from school at least once

T  F  was expelled from school at least once

T  F  was referred to DYS or DSS

## MILITARY SERVICE

**When serving in the military (if this applies) I was ...**

T  F  put on more disciplinary details than most

T  F  once demoted in rank

T  F  taken into custody by Military Police or Shore Patrol

T  F  put in the stockade

T  F  called before a military court

T  F  discharged early

T  F  discharged on medical or psychiatric grounds

T  F  given an other-than-honorable discharge

## ADULT SOCIAL ADJUSTMENT

**As an adult, I have ...**

T  F  been involved in an incident of shoving, grabbing, or hitting

T  F  been known as someone with a temper

T  F  enjoyed rough sex

T  F  taken items from a store

T  F  enjoyed gambling more than most people

T  F  taken money that wasn't mine

T  F  been the victim of harassment

T  F  been mugged

T  F  had my home broken into or my car stolen

**Figure 3.3.** Continued

---

T  F  been pursued by a bill collector

T  F  had something repossessed for nonpayment

T  F  had periods of no income

T  F  been in debt

T  F  declared bankruptcy

T  F  had to deal with a financial encumbrance such as alimony, child support, or a lien on property or income

## OCCUPATION

**Regarding my work history, I ...**

T  F  have gone without finding work for as long as three months

T  F  have been put on probation

T  F  have been fired

T  F  have had three or more jobs in the past two years

T  F  am overqualified for my present job

T  F  have generally been dissatisfied with my main occupation

**More than most of my coworkers, I have had to deal with ...**

T  F  being unable to get to work or being late

T  F  exceptionally high performance standards

T  F  hazing or harassment in the workplace

T  F  difficult clients or customers

T  F  negative attitudes of the public

**My real interests outside of work (hobbies) ...**

T  F  include activities involving risk

T  F  involve studying, collecting, or practicing with weapons

T  F  include reading *Soldier of Fortune* or similar magazines

T  F  include movies, videos, or books about combat

# **Figure 3.3.** Continued

---

| | | |
|---|---|---|
| T | F | tend to be neglected because of other responsibilities |
| T | F | are private, and not such that I wish to share with others |

## LEGAL ISSUES

**I have at some time been involved in legal proceedings around ...**

| | | |
|---|---|---|
| T | F | professional bill collection |
| T | F | repossession of property |
| T | F | bankruptcy |
| T | F | legal separation or divorce |
| T | F | a civil suit, either by or against someone else |

**Regarding brushes with the law, I have had ...**

| | | |
|---|---|---|
| T | F | more motor vehicle violations than most people I know |
| T | F | my driver's license suspended |
| T | F | a restraining order against me |
| T | F | protective custody |
| T | F | a court summons for a nontraffic violation |
| T | F | a criminal charge against me |
| T | F | a sentence against me (including a suspended sentence) |

## HEALTH

**Regarding physical health, I am sometimes bothered by ...**

| | | |
|---|---|---|
| T | F | shaking or trembling |
| T | F | hot flashes or chills |
| T | F | racing or pounding heart |
| T | F | feeling lightheaded or dizzy |
| T | F | frequent urination |
| T | F | nausea or gastric distress |
| T | F | stomach pain or bowel discomfort |

## Figure 3.3. Continued

| | | |
|---|---|---|
| T | F | constipation or diarrhea |
| T | F | dry mouth or difficulty swallowing |
| T | F | blurred vision |
| T | F | clammy hands or feet |
| T | F | shortness of breath |
| T | F | headache |
| T | F | pain or stiffness in my back, neck, or another part of my body |
| T | F | other problems |

**Regarding mental health, I ...**

| | | |
|---|---|---|
| T | F | sometimes feel so down that I can't get out of bed for several days |
| T | F | sometimes feel the future is unreal and hard even to imagine |
| T | F | sometimes doubt that life is worth living |
| T | F | am more sensitive and aware than most people |
| T | F | am moodier than most of my friends |
| T | F | find that others keep things from me because I get too upset |
| T | F | was told to see a counselor, but chose not to go |
| T | F | have been to see counselor or psychotherapist |
| T | F | have had other emotional problems than those listed above |
| T | F | have been prescribed medication for anxiety or depression |

**Regarding the use of alcohol and drugs, I ...**

| | | |
|---|---|---|
| T | F | sometimes have a drink to relax |
| T | F | occasionally smoke marijuana |
| T | F | have thought about cutting down on alcohol |
| T | F | have tried hard drugs in the past |
| T | F | could drink more than most people if I chose to |
| T | F | agree that a daily drink or two may be good for you |

**Figure 3.3.** Continued

| | | |
|---|---|---|
| T | F | have tried cocaine in the past |
| T | F | find a drink or two is a harmless way to unwind |
| T | F | know people who would say I drink too much |

ing clinical pathology led to an interest in their wider use to predict job success and analyze personnel problems. Psychologists and business management tried to use the familiar clinical instruments to deal with normal-range behaviors, with varying degrees of success. Certainly there is little question about the importance of detecting problems of serious psychopathology, in either a clinical or a work setting. However, what became apparent in the work environment was the clear need for specific measures of things like attention to detail, self-confidence, openness to new information, honesty, attitude toward supervision, likability, team-playing ability, independent functioning, congeniality, risk-taking, and expression of hostility.

In developing tests of these normal-range workplace performance criteria, there has been a great shift in emphasis away from psychological interpretation. The older tests focused on personality type and pathology as primary variable(s), from which secondary, job-related behaviors were predicted. The current generation of tests are focused on subjects' tendencies toward specific behaviors. Behavior-based test reports are much clearer and—since they are free of psychodynamic formulation—greatly reduce concerns about reporting private information to management when confidentiality is waived.

Even with a release, you must be careful not to include too much psychobabble or clinical information in the test report, because such information may be misinterpreted or misused by well-intentioned administrative personnel. You should simply address relevant job performance issues. When questions arise about serious impairment, you can modify the battery of tests to include more clinically focused instruments such as the *MMPI*, and the *Beck Depression Scale*, and intelligence or projective tests.

Often, an evaluation is recommended for the purpose of verifying an employee's "fitness for duty." Following a workplace incident, many companies place the involved employees on temporary leave until it has been determined that they are able to resume work. But assessment also may be requested for working employees with lesser performance problems. In either situation, tests can provide vital information about present and future job behaviors. The case study that follows provides a vivid example.

A veteran machine operator in a tool and die factory—a man long known as testy and mistrustful—has become the

---

1.   **Management/supervisory intake.** Talk with supervisors, management, union representatives, etc. regarding the behaviors that have taken place in the workplace. Gain an understanding of the specific concerns and questions relevant to the situation. Get background information on the individual as well as the organization.

2.   **Initial evaluation meeting.** Meet with the employee to orient him or her to the evaluation process, explain and complete the release-of-information form, and complete the psychological tests.

3.   **Secondary evaluation.** Meet with the employee again (after the psychological tests have been evaluated) and complete the structured interview

4.   **Postevaluation consultation.** Consult with supervisors or management regarding the results of the evaluation.

5.   **Written report.** Provide a summary of the results of the evaluation in a timely manner with limited psychobabble, making recommendations for the individual as well as the workplace.

6.   **Follow-up with employee.** Discuss with the employee the results of the evaluation and the recommendations made.

---

**Figure 3.4.** Outline of at-risk assessment procedure.

object of a rash of coworker complaints about verbal threats and menacing postures. Formerly considered merely unpleasant, he now is actually feared. The shop is in turmoil.

In addition to the usual assessment, the counselor performs a 90-minute battery of psychological tests and a follow-up interview. These reveal a profile of a personality-disordered man who is experiencing major stress because of family illness and chronic excessive drinking. He is in an acute state of anxiety and has a low tolerance for frustration, a high level of expressed anger, and a strong interest in weapons and guns.

However, the employee does not display the important violence indicators of thrill-seeking, disregard for rules, or social isolation. A potential for violence is judged to be present, but appears related to environmental stress and alcohol abuse rather than to antisocial personality features. Intervention with a program of organized alcohol recovery, personal therapy, and family counseling enables him to stabilize at his former level of performance and to maintain employment.

## THE ROLE OF PSYCHOLOGY CONSULTANTS

Although testing may focus on behavior and normal personality dynamics, indications of personality dysfunction may be derived through interpretation by a psychologist. Or, the chosen battery may be composed of more clinically focused instruments. Even when tests are computer-scored, psychologists can choose specific instruments and then interpret the canned results. Often, contradictory findings are reported; these require a more in-depth look at the computer-generated report. Further, test results should never stand alone. They should be evaluated in the context of:

- information derived in the interview process,

- management consultation,

- demographics of the work organization, and

- other information from security or background checks.

We recommend that mental health professionals who are not psychologists establish a relationship with a consulting psychologist who can facilitate the testing component.

Remember, we are in the infancy of truly understanding human behavior. It was not long ago when "deranged" people were said to be possessed by demons or evil spirits and were locked up in prisons or asylums for years. The formal study of the human psyche is little more than 100 years old. We have seen significant advances in this field, but predicting human behavior, especially violence, is a very difficult task.

# Chapter 4

# THE AT-RISK AND THE TOXIC WORKPLACE

## CHARACTERISTICS OF AT-RISK COMPANIES

While there is a great deal of concern these days about disgruntled employees "going off" in the workplace, statistics indicate that these incidents represent a relatively small percentage of workplace violence. Further, as suggested in chapter 2, we have only limited ability to accurately predict those individuals prone to hostility and when they may react. However, those companies that have seen hostile and violent incidents do share certain characteristics. These characteristics depend on whether the violence came from *outside* or from *within* the workplace. An awareness of these characteristics is helpful in assessing an organization's vulnerability to hostile or violent behavior. Of greater significance, *many of these characteristics can be changed* in order to limit the risk.

*An at-risk organization is one that is vulnerable to hostile or violent activities perpetrated from outside the organization.* Figure 4.1 summarizes the factors that make some organizations likely victims of externally generated violence. This type of violence usually is the result of robberies for the purpose of financial gain, not personal conflict.

## Public Access, Late Hours, and Cash on Hand

According to NIOSH, the taxicab industry has the highest risk for workplace homicide: Taxi drivers face a risk nearly 60 times higher than the national average. Taxi companies are followed by liquor stores, detective and protective services, gas stations, and jewelry stores. These industries provide a high degree of public access; they keep large sums of money on hand; and they often stay open evenings and nights, when the cover of darkness, lack of pedestrian traffic, and poor security systems make them tempting targets of criminal activity. While most retail businesses have taken steps to tighten security, limit access, and curtail the amount of cash available, they still are vulnerable to violent acts.

## Desirable Consumer Goods

In addition to cash, consumer goods such as alcohol, prescription drugs, and other items that are easy to carry and sell illegally

---

- Is a retail business
- Keeps cash on hand
- Offers public access
- Operates during evenings, nights, and holidays
- Has no or an inadequate security system
- Has a small number of customers at any given time
- Uses solo employees
- Is in an isolated location or located near a highway
- Handles consumer goods that are valued on the street or are easily fenced

---

**Figure 4.1.** Characteristics of at-risk workplaces.

are attractive to criminals. Businesses that must stay open evenings, nights, weekends, and holidays are more vulnerable because of the reduced number of people around to observe and intervene in illegal activity. Criminals use the protection of isolation and darkness to catch the organization unaware.

## Service Settings

According NIOSH, most nonfatal assaults occur in service settings such as hospitals and nursing homes. Health care patients commit an astonishing 48% of all nonfatal assaults in the workplace; another 20% are committed in health care settings by family, friends, and other nonemployees. Only 4% to 6% of the nonfatal assaults are the result of coworker-to-coworker interactions.

## Domestic Abuse at Work

Even businesses that don't serve the direct public must examine the issue of access. Increasingly the media has broadcast stories about domestic situations that resulted in violent episodes at work. Outraged lovers have been known to stalk employees at work, and even to enter the workplace to confront or kill them. If nonemployees have easy access to the interior of the workplace through unlocked doors and unstaffed and understaffed reception areas, the company is at-risk for violence from the outside.

Organizations should consider such measures as locked doors, ceiling-to-floor partitions, separation of work areas, security guards, identification badges, and camera surveillance. They need to make it more difficult for the public to enter the premises and access the workforce (see chapter 10). Keeping the workplace safe from uninvited interlopers is especially important when planning for the discharge of employees. At these times, the locations of human resources and executive offices should be carefully examined, because they are often the scenes of confrontation between disgruntled ex-workers and their employers.

Even when all these factors have been minimized or eliminated, companies may be at-risk for internal aggression—one employee using violence against another. In this situation, aggressive behavior may result from a "toxic" work environment.

## CHARACTERISTICS OF A
## TOXIC WORK ENVIRONMENT

As suggested in the introduction, the workplace of today is safer, more secure, and more comfortable than at any time in history. However, it also is true that the workplace of today is undergoing changes that often result in significant turmoil and transition. When workers are asked what constitutes a stressful workplace, most have no difficulty forming long lists. Unfortunately, most people employed outside the home have had direct experience with reorganization, downsizing, changes in technology, relocation, new bosses, new personnel policies, limitations of employee benefits, and other transitions in the workplace. However, what makes a toxic workplace is not so much *what* happens in it but *how it is handled*.

### Limited Opportunities, Poor Conditions, and Ineffective Management

As shown in Table 4.1, toxic workplaces are characterized by limited employment opportunities, poor working conditions, and ineffective management. In addition, many workers complain of indecisive leadership, unclear directives, an atmosphere of fear and blame, disrespect between employees and supervisors, and abusive bosses. All of these factors strongly affect worker productivity, morale, and behavior. As a result, organizations pay a higher cost to maintain a healthy workforce, and society bears the brunt of escalating fees for health care, antisocial behavior, and citizen apathy. No employer is immune to the financial and emotional burden of toxic workplaces.

People working in toxic environments are at greater risk for a variety of health problems, failing relationships, and addictive behaviors. They are more apt to become ill, get injured on the job, make mistakes, work inefficiently, and eventually leave. This trans-

**TABLE 4.1**
**Contributing Elements to Toxic Workplaces**

| Employment Options | Working Conditions | Management Style |
|---|---|---|
| Much change | Heavy workload | Withholding |
| Few jobs available | Large responsibilities | Authoritarian |
| New management | Overtime expected | Untrained |
| Low wages | Substandard facilities | Arbitrary decisions |
| Limited benefits | Inadequate resources | Inflexible |
| No upward mobility | Change of shifts | No communication |
| No job security | Unsupervised | Favoritism |
| Weekends required | No say in decisions | Inconsistent |
| Undesirable customers | No autonomy | Nepotism |

lates into higher costs of doing business because of absenteeism, workers' compensation claims, poor-quality goods and services, lower productivity, and high rates of turnover. In other words, a toxic work environment shrinks the bottom line. Such an atmosphere also may put a company at-risk for hostility and violence.

The majority of workers do their jobs and cope with the stresses of the modern-day workplace. People working under high stress, and those in toxic work environments, often are described as "disgruntled." As we noted in chapter 2, under high stress vulnerable individuals may act out their feelings in a wide variety of inappropriate ways, sometimes including hostile and violent acts.

The question that must be addressed is whether certain factors in a work organization might prompt a vulnerable individual to deal with his or her situation through hostile and violent means. The toxic workplace is a breeding ground for tensions and resentments that may precipitate inappropriate behavior. These workplaces are characterized by acts that appear unfair, take away privileges previously in place, or run counter to an employee's personal interest.

## Favoritism

Further, when an employer shows favoritism toward one person, workers are bound to feel upset. Such feelings also arise when decisions repeatedly go against certain individuals, or when benefits are limited or removed. The following case study shows how some simple changes resulted in a high level of toxicity and led to intense feelings of anger toward upper management and the owner of a small manufacturing company.

The ABC Manufacturing Company began as a mom-and-pop business that grew from the owner's garage to a large-scale operation in its first five years. The owner, who had limited formal education and certainly no training in business management, related to his employees on a very personal level. Like the father of a large family, he had favorites and he rewarded them, while ignoring others. Because it was important to be well-liked by all, he did institute company-wide rewards, such as Christmas turkeys, retreats to his summer cottage on the ocean, employee parties, and a good benefits package. Most importantly, he began giving $1,000 "loyalty awards" to employees who had been with the company for 10 years. After about 15 years of growth, the company began to plateau and sales started falling off. Many of the 100 or so employees had been with the company since its early days of growth.

By now the owner's wife was vice president; his son, who had no training or formal education, was plant manager; and his daughter was office manager. In an effort to cut costs, they made what they thought were sound business decisions. They eliminated the company Christmas party; instituted salary cuts ranging from 0% to 20%, depending on the family's relationship with the employee; eliminated the $1,000 bonus for long-time employees; and fired one long-term employee for "insubordination" when he spoke up about some of the changes.

Further, several long-term employees had difficulty working with the plant manager (the owner's son). When their attempts to deal with him directly became increasingly tense, they decided to speak with the owner himself. When approached, the owner listened attentively, reported the conversation to his wife and son, and did nothing to rectify the situation.

The employees felt that they had made the company what it was, and that they were being treated unfairly. The atmosphere became increasingly hostile, and formerly good workers began to detach and act out their feelings in passive-aggressive ways—calling in sick, taking long breaks, refusing to make decisions without the plant manager's approval, not communicating with each other or with management.

Although there was no overt violence, the workplace was charged with a palpable tension and high level of toxicity. Productivity and quality decreased, and customers were lost to competitors, leading to more cutbacks and eventually a layoff. Many long-time employees left to work for competitors. Within 18 months, the company was half its former size and struggling to survive. Six months later, it was purchased by one of its competitors. The owner and his wife retired. Shortly thereafter, the son was terminated from his position.

If an employer makes decisions fairly and compassionately, with an expression of genuine concern for workers and some measure of compensation, even layoffs and cutbacks can be received with a minimum of ill will. An example comes to mind of another family-held manufacturing company faced with the hard task of laying off almost one-third of its workforce in order to survive. Because its human resources manager treated employees with dignity and respect, informed them ahead of time about the necessary downsizing, and organized programs to retrain and help them find other employment, the workers responded with good will and a high level of productivity. As a result, despite the layoff, the company witnessed one of its best years economically and avoided any overtly hostile or violent behavior.

## Mistrust

Companies that have toxic atmospheres are characterized by suspicious relationships among workers, managers, and owners. At times, the suspicion extends to customers as well. Ryan and Oestreich (1991) labeled the phenomenon the *cycle of mistrust*. The system feeds on negative assumptions about the other players in the work arena, observations that reinforce the assumptions, and aggressive behaviors on which they are based. Once started, the cycle predictably sustains itself.

Employees in this cycle assume that no one is concerned about them, that managers are insensitive to their needs, and that they will be exploited to the maximum extent possible without acknowledgment or appropriate reward. If a manager asks about their ideas, feelings, and opinions, he or she does so only to appease them and has no intention of really listening or implementing suggested solutions. Employees perceive management as threatened by their competence. They assume that decision making takes place behind closed doors and outside the view of labor. Assuming a high degree of dishonesty in human interactions, employees believe that managers are capable of vindictiveness and retaliation.

With such a view of work life, employees must look out for themselves rather than for the organization. They learn to work to standard, meaning they do exactly what is required, no more and no less. They make sure to take the full time allotted for breaks, meals, and sick, personal, and vacation days. They withhold information unless specifically asked. Although they often fail to participate actively in meetings, they challenge any decision made. Rather than keep supervisors informed of potential problems, they wait until things go wrong and then blame circumstances, poor decision making, and faulty leadership. They make fun of the boss to coworkers and customers. Focusing primarily on their rights to better working conditions, salary, and benefits, they seek to join labor unions and file lawsuits.

Managers in this situation also harbor tainted perceptions about employees. They assume that workers must be prodded to do their jobs and care only for their paychecks. They perceive employees as feeling and acting with a sense of entitlement. They see workers constantly challenging policies, breaking rules, and testing the supervisors' patience to get out of doing their jobs. Managers assume that workers are incapable of grasping the big picture (especially budget information) and will take advantage of any ambiguous situation. With this perspective, individual employees must be carefully scrutinized and directed, lest they sabotage the job and set poor examples for the rest of the workforce.

## Micromanagement

Micromanagement is a predictable response to the cycle of mistrust. Managers must tell employees what to do and check constantly on how the job gets done. Supervisors must provide more rules and tighter enforcement. Moreover, the workplace needs a formal hierarchy to handle worker complaints. Given the limitations of their performance and view of the workplace, managers often feel they have no choice but to withhold information, gratification, privileges, acknowledgment, rewards, and participation in decision-making activities.

Not surprisingly, people get what they expect. Employees see supervisors who behave insensitively and inhumanely, without regard for feelings or responses; managers see inefficiencies, waste, and high overhead costs. In such a toxic setting, the quality and quantity of goods and services fail to reach an optimal level. All parties feel suspicious of one another, disappointed with the results, skeptical about the future, and justified in their behavior. As a result, the toxic atmosphere continues and often escalates.

## Theory X Management

Suspicious thinking often gives rise to scrutiny of the other party's behavior in order to protect one's self-interest and avoid being taken advantage of. Such behavior is consistent with *theory X management,* which posits that employees are disinclined to work and so must be forced to do so. Since employers know what must be done and how best to do it, they must give detailed instructions for each assignment and only that information which is needed at the moment. A disastrous outcome results: Workers become dependent on management and stop thinking for themselves. Gone are initiative, creativity, and genuine involvement with the task; they are replaced with submissiveness, passivity, and dependency.

Theory X management calls for close supervision of work. Unable to assume that workers are doing things right, managers must constantly scrutinize the work and tell employees when productivity declines, mistakes occur, and performance is substandard. Since the only feedback workers receive is disapproval, they respond by doing as little as possible to avoid more negative criticism. Supervisors then respond with even closer scrutiny and enforce the rules more tightly—which further restricts worker autonomy.

Other problems result. Efficiency dictates that supervisors group similar tasks together and assign specific workers to them. As employees become associated with a particular function, *they may be viewed as replaceable parts*. As a result, employees derive less satisfaction from their work and the level of stress increases.

As management and employees fail to meet one another's expectations, each side feels justified in withholding additional resources. Information is an initial casualty. Management reasons that employees can't get the big picture—that they lack the intelligence to comprehend, the perspective to understand, and the need to know what's happening in the business. So managers withhold such data as the income and expense lines, output figures, profit and loss statements, external market forces, and so forth. When considering cost-cutting measures, management usually excludes employees from discussions of possible layoffs, mergers, or closings of units, departments, or product lines.

Employees also withhold information. They seldom share their discontent, frustration, or criticism openly. Their thoughts about how work could be improved remain a secret. Instead, they complain among themselves, fueling more hostile feelings. Their energy and ideas, which could be harnessed into productive work and helpful change, go underground and become fertile ground for more distrust.

When management and employees converse, they often withhold respect. An atmosphere of mistrust, apprehension, and uncertainty permeates the exchange of information. Each side comes away from such encounters feeling demeaned and devalued. Thus a negative feedback loop is established in which management distrusts what workers are doing and workers suspect management's motives. As each party becomes more entrenched in its position, its behavior reinforces the other side's negative judgments and views.

Clearly, such distrust influences the relationships employees have with customers and vendors. If employees don't feel positive about their employer, it is difficult to represent the company otherwise to outsiders. Subsequently, such companies may see a decline in their sales, profits, and market shares. Now the downward spiral accelerates, and may result in serious financial reversals.

Downsizing the workforce often seems like the solution. Because of the mistrust, management excludes workers from discussions of this possibility. Yet rumors abound. No matter who is laid off, all employees feel betrayed and abandoned. Despite their loyalty to the job, their hard labor, and their sacrifice in accepting a less-than-ideal work environment, their contract with management is damaged.

For the remaining workers, the demand for productivity increases. Thus stress permeates the entire process of downsizing, from its first considerations through eventual layoffs to the resulting increased workloads on the survivors. Noer (1993) described the devastating process of corporate downsizing and its effect on personnel as being like warfare.

Lewis (1994) compared downsizing to undergoing surgery. The organization is hemorrhaging and extreme intervention is required. But even in medicine, when surgery is successful, the patient sometimes dies because of infection or insufficient postsurgical care. In the same way, an organization may survive downsizing but succumb to "postsurgery infection" and trauma if the surviving personnel do not receive good care. It is the toxicity that develops around these organizational crises that may prompt a troubled employee to become violent employee.

## SUMMARY

At what point does an employee become at-risk for violence? In what way does he or she express that hostility? On whom does the employee unload? These are questions that have no clear-cut answers; the answers depend on the individual's unique mix of previous socialization, history, maturity, personal stability, and current job stress. Only a small percentage of workers threaten or become openly violent.

Personal factors certainly must be taken into account, but a company's toxic atmosphere may ignite latent hostile tendencies and push over the edge those individuals vulnerable to acting out in inappropriate or hostile ways. It behooves employers to become familiar with the warning signs that often precede such behavior. Yet, the goal should not be to find the at-risk employee and dispose of him or her. Rather, the organization must take a close look at its own toxicity and find methods to limit it effects (see chapter 12).

# Chapter 5

# WARNING SIGNS

Violence can erupt when you least expect it. One day the owner of a group medical practice approached a colleague to discuss a decrease in business. She surmised that because this doctor had taken several vacation weeks over the past few months, some of his patients had stopped treatment or had found other clinicians. As she was explaining her observations, he suddenly raised his fist as if to strike her. Startled, she stepped aside, averting a potential blow, and the conversation ended. Upon reflection she realized what might have happened, and she resolved to terminate the doctor's use of the facilities. Much to her relief, he approached her first and tendered his resignation.

We might think that highly educated, professional people do not act out violently in the workplace. Yet news stories report otherwise. In March of 1998, a professional accountant shot his boss and coworkers at the headquarters of the Connecticut state lottery before taking his own life.

While we can't predict the boiling point for any given individual, behavior signs and attitude changes can alert an observant supervisor or coworker that something is wrong. We don't have to wait until the first blow is struck to begin addressing potentially dangerous situations in the workplace.

In this chapter we will examine general signs that indicate failing performance in the troubled employee. Then we'll review the signs that are highly correlated with hostile and violent behavior in the at-risk employee.

## OBSERVABLE CLUES

### Attendance Problems

As indicated in Figure 5.1, the most obvious clue of poor performance—*attendance problems*—can take many forms. Most managers know that a pattern of absenteeism invariably points to a problem. So they often are suspicious of absences that occur immediately before or after paydays, weekends, holidays, shutdowns, and vacations. Yet they also must identify more subtle patterns, such as arriving late, leaving early, or using unscheduled time (especially vacation days) in the middle of the week. Other absences include being away from the work station for frequent restroom, coffee, and smoking breaks; being unaccountably missing for pe-

---

- Is absent before and after paydays, weekends, and holidays
- Frequently is absent for minor illnesses, such as colds, flu, or upset stomach
- Uses unscheduled vacation time
- Often requests personal time off
- Is often late to work
- Often leaves work early
- Frequently is missing from work station
- Management and coworkers have difficulty locating person

---

**Figure 5.1.** Failing attendance: Warning signs.

- Misses deadlines
- Uneven performance (yo-yo)
- Inefficiency; work requires more effort and time
- Inconsistent quality
- Faulty judgments
- Poor decision making
- Lapses in concentration
- Failure to remember instructions
- Inability to recall mistakes

**Figure 5.2.** Poor work: Warning signs.

riods of time throughout the workday; spending a lot of time with coworkers; and not showing up for scheduled assignments.

## Performance Problems

Attendance problems clearly cause declines in productivity. If employees are not present on the job, they cannot get their work done. As shown in Figure 5.2, besides absenteeism managers often notice other signs of poor performance, such as missing deadlines, uneven performance, poor judgment, faulty decision making, and inattentiveness. Troubled employees may be unable to think clearly or to concentrate, or they may be preoccupied with personal concerns. This, in turn, leads to forgetting directions and making mistakes. The result of any of these symptoms is inefficiency, poor quality of work, and uneven performance.

## Risky Behavior

Another warning sign of a troubled employee is frequent participation in unsafe conduct. Figure 5.3 lists the various consequences of failing to heed safety procedures. Equipment breaks down, property is damaged or destroyed, and people get injured, maimed, or even killed.

- • Takes risks
- • Violates safety procedures
- • Disregards other people's welfare
- • Has accidents resulting in
  - wasted materials
  - equipment failure
  - property damage
  - injury

**Figure 5.3.** Unsafe conduct: Warning signs.


## Mood Swings and Socially Unacceptable Behavior

The major tell-tale sign of potential hostility and violence can be seen in how workers relate to one another. Most supervisors balk at judging how people interact. Figure 5.4 lists a wide variety of alterations in mood and conduct a manager can watch for. The key is to become aware of any change from what is normal for a worker. Extremes in mood—happiness, sadness, anger, anxiety, aloofness—may suggest an aberration and should be monitored. Usually such changes are accompanied by complaints from those who have contact with the employee. Friction between coworkers escalates, and the ability to get along diminishes.

A manager should make note of any of the unacceptable behaviors listed in Figure 5.5. Arriving at or returning to work under the influence of alcohol or other drugs is especially dangerous, as violence is highly correlated with drug abuse. Moreover, drugs curtail physical coordination, mental acuity, and judgment. The use of any mood-altering drug can increase the potential for hostile and violent acts. Like substance use, emotional instability should heighten a manager's alertness for problems. The commitment to providing a safe workplace dictates that we cannot ignore people who act in peculiar ways.

## VERBAL CLUES

### Denial or Minimizing of Problems

Most of the warning signs listed above can be observed visually. But what often clinches the suspicion for supervisors or coworkers is the message they *hear* from the troubled employee. Often the individual denies a problem. As seen in Table 5.1, denial can take many forms, the simplest of which is the statement, "Not me." When asking a troubled employee about his or her attendance, performance, conduct, relationships, or behavior, the manager must listen closely to hear if the individual takes responsibility for his or her actions. He or she may minimize the extent or frequency of the problem or blame circumstances or other people, especially the immediate supervisor, management, and larger organization. By listening carefully, a supervisor can hear the individual distort evidence, rationalize or justify conduct, change the subject, or offer a litany of excuses.

---

- Imagined problems between others

- Complaints from coworkers, customers, or vendors

- Friction with coworkers

- Avoidance of people

- Overreaction to criticism

- Wide mood swings

- Negative attitude

- Depression, crying jags

- Irritability

- High anxiety

- Hostility

- Inability to get along with others, especially when he or she used to

---

**Figure 5.4.** Impaired relationships: Warning signs.

- Unacceptable personal appearance
- Neglect of hygiene
- Temper tantrums
- Physical violence
- Emotional outbursts
- High on alcohol or other drugs

**Figure 5.5.** Unacceptable behaviors: Warning signs.

**Not Now.**    A more subtle means of denial is the "not now" approach. The person admits that a problem may have existed in the past; however, by correcting the mistake, he or she denies the existence of the problem in the present. What makes this form of denial so challenging is that the supervisor often gets sidetracked; instead of focusing on the ongoing nature of the problem, he or she only sees that it is currently in abeyance. It doesn't exist at this moment in time. A results-oriented supervisor can easily miss this warning sign because the situation has been momentarily rectified.

An example of this is the employee who *had* a drinking problem, entered an inpatient program for seven days, and returned to work. The supervisor might dismiss prior wrongdoing now that he or she knows the individual is taking care of the matter. Often, however, simply "putting down the drink" does not mean the problem is resolved; it only indicates that the person has taken the initial step to recovery. Job performance and personal problems still may be issues the supervisor must handle in a direct and supportive manner.

**Never Again.**    Another form of denial is the infamous pledge: "Never again." The employee promises that the problem has been solved permanently; yet, he or she continues to deny responsibility for its occurrence in the first place. Most supervisors want to hear the "never again" oath because it seems to fix the problem

## Table 5.1
## Employee Statements of Denial

| Not me | Not now | Never again |
|---|---|---|
| I didn't do it. I'm not responsible. | Don't worry; It's fixed (or will be shortly). | I promise this is the last time. |
| It's not my fault. He provoked me. | What's the big deal? It's working now. | I'm sure it won't ever happen again. |
| I'm not the only one. She's much worse. | It isn't that bad. | I know I've turned the corner. |
| You didn't tell me to do it that way. | I've already explained what happened. | I know better now. |

now and forever. As with all types of denial, however, unless the individual takes ownership of the behavior that gave rise to the performance issue, nothing will change. The person must accept the problem before he or she can make any guarantees. Simply *admitting* there is a problem is not the same as *accepting* the problem. Accepting a problem connotes responsibility for the situation as well as an understanding of the impact it has had on one's life. The supervisor and the employee both must recognize that the process of recovery takes time and patience.

### NONVERBAL CLUES

While managers and coworkers must listen closely to a troubled employee's words, volume, tone, and accompanying body language can communicate far more clearly whether the worker is at-risk for hostile or violent behavior. The nonverbal clues listed below all carry important weight in determining risk:

- an edge to the tone of voice
- mumbling responses
- failing to look the other person in the eyes

"shifty" eye contact

a blank stare

wringing the hands

pacing

making threatening gestures

## Gut-Level Warnings

There is a final and critical cue supervisors and coworkers receive from interacting with a potentially hostile and dangerous person: *how they feel in the encounter.* In Figure 5.6 we have listed some gut feelings that indicate something is not right.

Supervisors often report higher stress levels when they feel compelled to watch what they say or how they act around the individual. It's like walking on egg shells. They are concerned about

---

- Stressed

- Burdened

- Cautious and uncertain, like "walking on egg shells"

- Sympathetic and compassionate

- Conned; taken advantage of

- Disappointed; let down

- Angry, frustrated, or enraged

- Guilty

- Inadequate

- Overwhelmed

- Confused

---

**Figure 5.6.** Gut reactions and feelings of supervisors that may be warning signs.

upsetting the person and so take greater care in their language and actions. In addition, the supervisor may assume full responsibility for the outcome and accept the guilt for anything that goes awry.

While managers and coworkers may be aware of their own anger, they also may feel sympathy or compassion for the troubled employee, thus compounding their own sense of guilt. Feeling out of control or overwhelmed by the situation also leads to confusion and an ability to cope. At the same time, the supervisor often wants to disown such feelings and believe that the interaction is normal. "Monday morning quarterbacking" is a common characteristic of many supervisor-employee discussions. The "woulda, coulda, shoulda" routine often accompanies any replay of the discussion. As we'll see in chapter 6, supervisor training is an essential ingredient in limiting this stressful phenomenon.

## MAINTAINING OBJECTIVITY

While the broad indicators listed above might point to a potential for hostility or violence, they also might suggest other problems. An organization protects itself best from legal consequences by noting general performance factors rather than specifying those related to hostile or violent behavior. Using a checklist like the one shown in Figure 5.7 can help. For reasons of objectivity and fairness, two or more observers should be engaged. If a company is unionized, management should ask the steward to help complete the form. Remember that the presence of warning signs does not lead to a definitive assessment or diagnosis. The organization should leave that to a professional psychologist or counselor who is trained in using such observations and gathering additional information to determine risk.

Table 5.2 lists behaviors that may indicate risk for hostility and violence. These include the use of alcohol and other mood-altering drugs, unsafe conduct, negative attitudes, hostile moods, lingering anger, denial, threatening words, threatening gestures,

*(Text continues on page 78.)*

**Figure 5.7.** Checklist of potential warning signs.

|  | Yes | No |
| --- | :---: | :---: |
| **Quality and Quantity of Work** | | |
| Clear refusal to do assigned tasks | ___ | ___ |
| Significant increase in errors | ___ | ___ |
| Repeated errors in spite of increased guidance | ___ | ___ |
| Inconsistent, up-and-down quantity and quality of work | ___ | ___ |
| Behavior that disrupts workflow | ___ | ___ |
| Procrastination on significant decisions or tasks | ___ | ___ |
| More than usual amount of supervision required | ___ | ___ |
| Frequent, unsupported explanations for poor work | ___ | ___ |
| Noticeable change in written or verbal communication | ___ | ___ |
| Other, specify: _____ | ___ | ___ |
| **Interpersonal Relationships** | | |
| Significant change in relations with inside workers | ___ | ___ |
| Significant change in relations with outside people | ___ | ___ |
| Frequent or intense arguments | ___ | ___ |
| Verbal abusiveness (yelling, cursing, racial/ethnic slurs, etc.) | ___ | ___ |
| Physical abusiveness (pushing, hitting, threatening, etc.) | ___ | ___ |
| Persistently withdrawn or less involved | ___ | ___ |
| Intentional avoidance of supervisor or manager | ___ | ___ |
| Extreme expressions of frustration or discontent | ___ | ___ |
| Change in frequency or nature of complaints | ___ | ___ |
| Complaints by coworkers or outside people | ___ | ___ |
| Expressions of distrust of human nature | ___ | ___ |
| Unusual sensitivity to advice or feedback | ___ | ___ |
| Unpredictable response to guidance | ___ | ___ |
| Passive-aggressive attitude or behavior | ___ | ___ |

# Figure 5.7. Continued.

| | | |
|---|---|---|
| Doing things behind the back of supervisor | ___ | ___ |
| Other, specify _____ | ___ | ___ |

## General Job Performance

| | | |
|---|---|---|
| Excessive absences | ___ | ___ |
| Unauthorized absences | ___ | ___ |
| Frequent Monday/Friday absences or other pattern | ___ | ___ |
| Unexplained disappearances | ___ | ___ |
| Frequent extended breaks | ___ | ___ |
| Frequent early departure from work | ___ | ___ |
| Concern about or actual incidents of safety offenses | ___ | ___ |
| Experiences or causes accidents on the job | ___ | ___ |
| Breakage, spillage, or wasted materials | ___ | ___ |
| Interferes with or ignores established procedures | ___ | ___ |
| Inability to correct performance | ___ | ___ |
| Other, specify _____ | ___ | ___ |

## Personal Conduct

| | | |
|---|---|---|
| Changes in or unusual personal appearance | ___ | ___ |
| Changes in or unusual speech (volume, rate, pitch) | ___ | ___ |
| Changes in or unusual physical mannerisms | ___ | ___ |
| Changes in or unusual facial expressions | ___ | ___ |
| Changes in or unusual level of activity (up or down) | ___ | ___ |
| Talks about death, suicide, or harming someone | ___ | ___ |
| Irritability | ___ | ___ |
| Disruptive behavior | ___ | ___ |
| Tearfulness | ___ | ___ |
| Fearful, paranoid | ___ | ___ |
| Careless, carefree, "throws caution to the wind" | ___ | ___ |

**Figure 5.7.** Continued.

| | | |
|---|---|---|
| Talks about obtaining or using alcohol or other drugs | ___ | ___ |
| Makes unfounded accusations about others | ___ | ___ |
| Secretive | ___ | ___ |
| Memory lapses, faulty concentration | ___ | ___ |
| Comes to work with alcohol on breath | ___ | ___ |
| Excessive fatigue | ___ | ___ |
| Makes unreliable or false statements | ___ | ___ |
| Unrealistic self-appraisal or boastfulness | ___ | ___ |
| Temper tantrums or angry outbursts | ___ | ___ |
| Demanding, rigid, inflexible | ___ | ___ |

verbal abuse, physical abuse, and a history of violence. The manager may have access to and should examine the employee's personnel record for a history of formal disciplinary actions. In its second column, Table 5.2 lists company circumstances that may heighten organizational stress and toxicity and thus affect the individual's personal stress. These include layoffs, mergers, changes in the reporting structure, decreased benefits, and relocations.

Finally, unless the organization and its individual managers have a firm understanding of what to do if they suspect the risk of violent behavior, knowing these signs will only escalate people's fears and reduce the possibility of maintaining a safe workplace. Supervisors must be trained not only to *recognize* the warning signs but to *respond* to the individual, using the resources available within the organization.

## TABLE 5.2
## Summary of At-Risk Factors

| Individual | Organizational |
|---|---|
| Use of alcohol | Layoffs |
| Use of mood-altering drugs | Mergers |
| Unsafe conduct | Change in supervision |
| Lingering negative attitude | Change in management |
| Lingering anger | Reduction in compensation |
| Denial | Reduction in benefits |
| Threatening words | Relocation |
| Threatening gestures | Change in employee demographics |
| Sexual harassment | |
| Verbal abuse | |
| Physical abuse | |
| Record of disciplinary actions | |

# Chapter 6

# THE THREE Ps: POLICIES, PROCEDURES, PROGRAMS

Today's organizations are beginning to see the need for changes in the workplace to lower the risk of hostility and violence. Forward-thinking companies have instituted a number of safety-minded practices that not only combat workplace hostility but also improve working conditions for all employees, thus lowering the degree of toxicity.

## ZERO-TOLERANCE POLICY (ZTP) FOR HOSTILITY

Following the philosophy and framework of antiharassment and antidiscrimination policies, organizations today are developing statements affirming that no form of hostility or violence will be tolerated in the workplace. In earlier days, an individual could not make a sexual, religious, or racially offensive comment, but he or she could threaten to do bodily harm without receiving disciplinary actions at work. A zero-tolerance policy (ZTP) covers all forms of offensive language and behavior in the workplace, regardless of its focus.

However, there is a downside to such a policy. As is the case with sexual harassment policies and those protecting against discrimination, this policy includes what many would consider humor, joking, or fooling around. A ZTP for violence prohibits even jokes and nonserious threats between two friends. The common, "I'll kill you!" or "I'll kick your butt!" could be subject to at least an investigation and possibly even disciplinary action if the policy were to be enforced as written.

Clearly, a policy that prohibits hostility and violence is an essential component to any proactive approach to maintaining a safe work environment. However, as with many new policies and procedures, there may be situations in which the policy is misinterpreted or used to manipulate others. An example of this would two friends joking about a bet they have made on an upcoming sporting event. One says to the other, "If I lose any more money to you, I'll just have to take a contract out on your life." This is overheard by another employee, who reports it as a threat of violence. Later it is determined that his ulterior motive is to discredit the "threatening" employee.

All ZTPs should include:

- Avoidance of subjective, vaguely defined terms such as *inappropriate*, *respectful*, and *negative*, as these are open to judgment calls.

- Clear definitions of specific types of behavior that will not be tolerated, such as hitting, fighting, spitting, yelling, swearing, or pushing, in jest or otherwise.

- Guidelines of how employees should report an incident and the steps that will be followed after a report is made.

- Clear answers to these questions:

  Who conducts the investigation?

  What is the process?

Who will have access to the information?

What legal rights do the parties have?

What are the potential repercussions of the outcome?

Companies must conduct mandatory educational seminars on zero tolerance for hostility. Figure 6.1 shows a sample ZTP for hostility.

## Figure 6.1. Sample ZTP for hostility.

It is the goal of the ABC Corporation to provide a physically and emotionally safe work environment. It is imperative that all employees, at every level, be treated with respect and dignity, regardless of race, nationality, religion, gender, age, sexual orientation, or position within the organization. To this end, we are implementing this policy to assist in clarifying behavioral and procedural expectations.

**Definitions of Hostility and Violence:** *Hostility* refers to any nonphysical form of harassment, discrimination, or offensive behavior. Examples include but are not limited to:

- ethnic, sexual, or racial jokes;

- verbal threats or offensive gestures;

- swearing at an individual;

- stalking or harassing phone calls.

*Violence* is any behavior—such as hitting, kicking, pushing, spitting, or biting—that results in unwanted physical contact or damage to property. Unwanted sexual contact is certainly considered hostile and violent behavior. There may be other behaviors that do not fall within these definitions that are also inappropriate for the workplace.

**Investigation Process:** It is expected that any employee experiencing or witnessing this type of behavior will make a report to (*personnel, security, human resources, etc.*). The alleged incident will be evaluated and investi-

**Figure 6.1.** Continued.

gated by *(safety, personnel, human resources)*. Also, if a union member is involved, the *(union official, steward, etc.)* will be notified immediately of the incident and of the investigation. If required, local law enforcement will be contacted.

Pending the results of the full investigation, the individual(s) involved may be

allowed to continue to work;

placed on administrative leave;

referred for a medical or psychological evaluation;

taken into the custody of the law enforcement agency; or

placed on some other administrative status.

**Confidentiality of Investigation:**   Every effort will be made to respect the confidentiality of all involved parties. However, this may not always be possible to guarantee, given the nature of the investigation. There may be occasions when other employees and witnesses must be interviewed about the alleged event or the alleged perpetrator's behavior. Should a referral to the EAP or a medical/psychological professional be indicated, a waiver of confidentiality will be requested in order for the investigating party to receive the results of the evaluation.

**Disciplinary Action:**   Upon completion of the investigation—which may include a medical or psychological evaluation as well a police investigation—a decision will be made regarding discipline. Hostile or violent behavior may result in disciplinary action up to and including termination of employment.

The goal of this policy is to prevent incidents from occurring, or from escalating if they do occur. It is not the intent of this policy to infringe on the rights of any employee, but to ensure respectful behavior. Further, the goal is to do everything possible to ensure a safe work environment for all personnel at all levels. It also should be noted that any parties involved in an alleged incident have the right to seek legal counsel at their own expense.

## Labor-Management Partnership

In organizations with unions, it is essential that labor and management work together to formulate policies and procedures. When crisis teams are developed, it is helpful to draw members from all parts of the organization. If possible, this joint effort should not be subject to the formalized labor-management relationship, but should stand as an independent team. Corporate politics being what they are, this may not always be possible; but many organizations have modeled this team approach in their safety committee meetings.

## EMPLOYEE ASSISTANCE PROGRAMS (EAPs)

An employee assistance program (EAP) is a vital tool in combating workplace hostility. The EAP provides the following services to an organization:

1. consultation to management when the company is faced with a difficult employee;

2. immediate assessment and referral of troubled employees;

3. a clearinghouse of information, research, policies, and procedures on relevant issues in the workplace;

4. input into policies and procedures for the company; and

5. training programs and seminars for employees on work-related issues.

A good EAP takes into account the corporate culture, employee demographics, politics, and policies of an organization. See chapter 9 for a detailed description of employee assistance programs.

## Supervisor Training

Today's supervisor often must manage employees who are anxious, agitated, and angry about changes at work. He or she may have to ask people to do more with less—especially after a downsizing. Employees may be feeling scared, upset, disgruntled, undervalued, unappreciated, and demoralized. As one supervisor exclaimed, "I not only have to get the work out, I have to be a junior 'shrink' as well!"

Most supervisors are promoted from within the ranks of an organization. A few come with business school training. However, few programs offer much training in people skills, communicating with employees, dealing with morale problems, or coping with an angry employee. Most of this is left to human resources, but it is the supervisor who must deal with these issues on a daily basis. Supervisors often are in the untenable position of having much responsibility but little authority.

Supervisory training is a key element in any violence-prevention program. Training supervisors in what to look for and how to address troubled employees is critical. Courses on communication, conflict resolution, stress management, and team building also are valuable to the supervisor of today, who is faced with an ever-changing workplace and workers feeling more and more stress.

## PROGRESSIVE DISCIPLINARY POLICIES (PDPs)

Disciplining an employee is stressful for everyone involved, yet supervisors often receive little or no training in this. A PDP provides a structured format by which a supervisor responds to an employee's job performance issues.

Most PDPs offer three levels of intervention: verbal, written, and administrative:

1.  Verbal intervention is the first step of the disciplinary process. The supervisor meets with the employee and discusses job performance difficulties and recommendations for their remediation. The supervisor should keep clear notes on the intervention and explain to the employee that the next step will be a written warning, if the difficulties are not addressed.

2. The written warning is the next step of intervention. Once again, the supervisor meets with the employee and outlines the specific job performance difficulties along with recommendations. At this point, the supervisor should refer the employee to the EAP. All of this should be written down, with a copy given to the employee. A follow-up session should be scheduled in order to monitor the employee's progress.

3. The administrative level is reached if the employee does not respond to verbal or written warnings and the problem continues. Typically at this point, some time has passed, recommendations have been made, and the employee's performance remains impaired. Usually there is some kind of administrative response, ranging from suspension to termination.

A PDP gives the supervisor a consistent intervention process, while assuring employees that there is a fair, system-wide procedure. A PDP requires the supervisor to assess job performance difficulties, not personality quirks or idiosyncrasies. The problem behaviors must be observable and documentable. Although subjectivity is always a factor, a good PDP will limit this variable. An observation worksheet, like the one described in chapter 5, should be used to help supervisors remain consistent.

## OTHER NECESSARY POLICIES

### Preemployment Screening and Hiring

A small business owner recalled a threatening incident involving an employee she had hired some months earlier. She had conducted an interview and checked the applicant's references before offering him the job. Much to her surprise and frustration, not only did he fail to work up to standard, he became quite hostile when she offered him feedback. Eventually she let him go for poor performance, putting up with a lot of verbal abuse along the way.

What happened next she never would have predicted. The fired employee began stalking her at work and home. He watched her enter and leave her workplace each day. She saw his parked car across the street when she visited customers. When she contacted the police, she found that her options were limited.

To this day she wonders whether he'll appear suddenly around the corner or approach her when she returns home. While the man has never become physically violent, the hostile work environment he created continues to haunt this businesswoman and affect her activities and her life.

Screening out potentially hostile or violent employees makes sense as an important first measure in ensuring a safe, productive, and humane workplace. Just a few years ago, it was difficult to ask for and receive much relevant information on a potential employee. Application forms and interviews were limited in terms of the questions they could ask. Past employers faced significant limitations on what they could disclose about an employee; often, they were able only to indicate if the person was eligible for rehire. The decision to hire usually was based on the gut feeling of the interviewer.

Today, however, there are new and improved ways of finding information on potential hires, including these:

1. Many organizations today contract with outside agencies to conduct preemployment screenings. These agencies often are better skilled at screening out potentially troublesome employees than most business managers. Many have developed screening procedures that utilize psychological tests under the supervision of a psychologist. Previously such agencies were brought in only to screen upper-level management personnel.

2. With the advent of computer scoring, companies can now administer psychological testing to potential hires at all levels. Some of these instruments can be used by human resource personnel. But it's even better to bring in a psy-

chologist who is trained to administer and interpret the results of the screening instrument.

3. Getting background information on a potential employee's driving, military, credit, work, and criminal record provides valuable information.

4. Learning good interviewing skills is essential. Very few managers receive training on how to interview a new employee. Usually they simply review the person's resume, tell him or her about the job, and ask about his or her skills. Today, human resource personnel are trained to *listen* to potential employees and to ask questions that elicit answers demonstrating *interpersonal style* and the applicant's ability to *communicate*. For example, the interviewer might pose a scenario that places the applicant in the middle of an interpersonal conflict and watch how he or she handles the situation.

5. Some forward-thinking companies now use input from employees as part of the hiring process. Who better to tell if someone will be a good fit than employees who work in the same department in similar positions? Participating employees must be screened and educated about their roles, but their perspective can be invaluable. Further, they may be more inclined to help the new employee adjust if they have this connection to him or her. If employee participation in the screening and hiring process is too political for an organization, employees may participate in the orientation program for a new employee.

## Employee Orientation and Handbook

Many companies offer new employees only limited orientation and training programs. Certainly, companies are required to post certain policies covering discrimination, harassment, and drug and alcohol involvement. Many organizations have beautifully designed and well-crafted mission statements posted in lobbies that purport lofty ideals and philosophies. However, they may have little direct discussion with new employees about policies on appropriate workplace dress, behavior, and language. We recommend that companies include these issues in their orientation processes, and also develop employee handbooks that review all aspects of behavioral expectations. Such handbooks should list the procedures the company will follow should an employee become the victim or perpetrator of any inappropriate behavior.

## Employee Surveys/Evaluations

In the 1980s, most American managers became familiar with the concept of *total quality management (TQM)*. Initially found in the Japanese workplace, it quickly became part of the corporate nomenclature of this country. As a result of Deming's influence, the hierarchical model of decision making gave way to team-derived decisions and strategy development. Task teams, cross-functional teams, and multidisciplinary teams were formed in a number of industries that required rapid response to the ever-changing marketplace and customer services. A byproduct of this model was an evaluation process by which all members of the team got to rate the efficacy of their proposals and working relationships.

Although many now question whether TQM has survived the downsizing of the American workplace, many of its influences remain. One is the idea of *surveying workers* to determine their morale and attitude. When employees have a forum for expressing their concerns, they tend to have lower levels of frustration. Certainly, companies must provide a level of safety, so employees trust they will not be punished for their candid feedback. Employee assistance personnel or outside consultants can help design and evaluate such a survey. It is important to report the results back to employees, along with any responses to the survey. Most importantly, these surveys must not become black holes, into which suggestions, feedback, information, and comments simply disappear, never to be heard from again.

Another concept beginning to change attitudes in the workplace is the *360-degree evaluation process*. The usual evaluation of an employee's job performance take places once a year, and his or her immediate supervisor does the evaluating. The employee might have input into the evaluation insofar as he or she agrees or disagrees with it. In the 360-degree evaluation the supervisor evaluates the employee, *and the employee evaluates the supervisor.* This works best in large departments in which employee-to-supervisor evaluations are done anonymously; general feedback is then given to the supervisor, without reference to specific individuals. This allows employees to comment on their supervisor's management and interpersonal skills as well as any areas of concern.

### Termination Policies and Services

In many organizations, there is no consistency in how different managers handle the same situations; therefore, there is a need for uniform policies and processes. In addition to progressive discipline, organizations should have a policy in place on termination of employees, whether by downsizing or reorganization or for disciplinary reasons.

First, the organization should review its current policies and how they are implemented. In the 1980s, when many large computer firms were faced with layoffs, the issues of security and employee sabotage loomed large. Many companies implemented termination procedures that were toxic in nature. Employees would be brought into a conference room, informed of their termination, and escorted by security to their offices to clean out their belongings. Then they were shown to the front door. This may have limited the company's risk from disgruntled employees, but it certainly demoralized the remaining workers, which eventually caused more harm than sabotage could have.

Most employees can identify with any worker who is experiencing a difficult situation at work. They watch to see how others are treated in any situation, and the company's conduct in response to one individual can have a dramatic effect on an entire department or company. In times of crisis, gossip and rumors often are the only consistent forms of communication. Therefore, consistency, courtesy, and kindness are essential when managing employees in difficult situations. Furthermore, consistent guidelines for terminating employees provide important protection against wrongful termination litigation.

Other strategies for individual or group termination are listed below:

- Provide exit interviews for employees leaving the company.

- Be sure employees know of the company's EAP.

- Have a system of follow-up contact with employees after they leave.

- Know and understand the dynamics of the organizational culture.

## AT-RISK PSYCHOLOGICAL EVALUATIONS

When an employee manifests behavior in the workplace that is inappropriate or worrisome, management and coworkers typically become concerned about safety, work performance, and disciplinary issues. If an organization has an EAP in place, the individual may be referred for assessment. However, the situation may be so difficult that more extensive and comprehensive evaluation is required. As described in chapter 3, this assessment should include:

A. A clinical interview that includes an assessment of

1. the incident from the individual's perspective;

2. a psychosocial history;

3. a review of current and past employment history; and

4. an evaluation of risk factors (see chapter 2).

B.  An extensive battery of psychological tests, including

    1.    paper-and-pencil psychometric tests, such as the *MMPI*, the *Millon,* or the *Clinical Analysis Questionnaire*;

    2.    projective tests, such as the *Rorschach* or the *Thematic Apperception Test (TAT)*; and

    3.    if indicated, intelligence and neurological screening.

C.  A detailed report presenting the findings in clearly understood terms, along with specific work recommendations. The report should be limited in how much personal information is revealed in order to protect the individual.

It goes without saying that this must include a signed release from the employee. The EA professional moves between the roles of clinician and consultant to facilitate the transition of the employee back into the workplace.

## Potential Conflicts with Civil Rights Laws

DiLorenzo and Carroll (1995) summarized the dilemma facing corporate America this way: *While responding to concerns about workplace hostility through screenings, evaluations, and profiling, the civil rights of all employees must be protected.* The Americans with Disabilities Act (ADA) mandates that employees with emotional disabilities not be discriminated against or harassed. Therefore, even if an employee seems to fit a potentially violent profile, there must be some indication of direct threat before a company can act on the basis of a profile or psychiatric category. Employers must ask five questions in determining if an employee poses a direct threat:

1.  Does the person pose a significant risk of substantial harm?

2.  Is the risk specific to the individual?

3. Is the risk specific to the current circumstances?

4. Is the risk based on objective evidence?

5. Can the risk be reduced through reasonable accommodation?

The answers to these questions can help determine if a risk is highly probable based on the current situation, not on speculation, stereotypes, rumors, or heresay. Furthermore, there must be documented evidence of potential risk; this means that medical and mental health professionals should be brought in to assess the individual and his or her level of disability and risk. In addition, the organization must make every effort to determine if the direct threat can be diminished by reasonable accommodation, such as reassignment.

On the other hand, companies may be legally liable for negligent hiring or retention if they knowingly hire or retain an employee who is unfit for work. The issue is a difficult one and is currently being dealt with in the legal system. We suggest that companies maintain incident response teams, conduct thorough background checks, establish a reporting and investigation system, and institute EAPs.

## CRISIS INTERVENTION TEAMS

Crises do occur with increasing regularity in the American workplace. Accidents, injuries, violent altercations, and employee deaths all have dramatic effects on employees and on the workplace. Many large organizations today have put together cross-functional teams to respond to the emotional turmoil generated by these kinds of incidents. The crisis intervention team should be representative of the entire organization, including personnel from labor, management, and administration. The team can respond to any situation directly or can gather appropriate resources to do so. The company should make sure this team receives training and consultation.

## SUMMARY

Combating workplace hostility requires a comprehensive effort at all levels. Too often, managers play "blame game" instead, or the goal becomes getting rid of the "bad apple." Often, it is obvious in retrospect that the situation could have been managed differently at an earlier stage, so that the situation got resolved. Unfortunately, there are times when an employee must be disciplined or even terminated from employment. We hope the strategies presented in this chapter will decrease the number of these instances.

# Chapter 7

# MANAGEMENT TRAINING

Once a policy and procedures have been written, the organization has the responsibility to inform supervisors. Front-line supervisors are best suited to prevent workplace violence for two reasons. First, they observe employee attitudes, behavior, and conduct on a daily basis. With proper training and guidance, they can identify changes that may be predictors of hostility and violence. Second, because they interact immediately and directly with workers, they have the first opportunity to intervene and defuse the situation. Another reason for focusing on front-line supervisors is this: If they don't have the knowledge and skills they need, they can unwittingly activate or escalate a violent response.

Figure 7.1 lists areas in which supervisors need training: recognizing warning signs, evaluating performance, knowing intervention and treatment resources, mediating, and communicating clearly. Naturally, they should be informed about the company's policies and procedures. Most of all, supervisors must know the importance of intervening at the first sign of a problem to avoid the high costs of lawsuits, destruction of property, and personal injury.

---

- Company policy of zero tolerance

- Definition of hostility and violent behavior

- Indicators of disgruntled employees

- Supervisor's role in responding to

     1. suspicious circumstances

     2. a crisis

- Role of employee assistance personnel

- Communication skills

- Conflict management skills

---

**Figure 7.1.** Content of management training.

Executives, managers, human resources personnel, medical staff, and union representatives also should receiving training in preventing hostility and violence (see Figure 7.2). In addition, executives, outside salespeople, and other employees who travel need to know about personal safety.

## ATTITUDE COUNTS

The issue of violence in the workplace is fraught with denial. Few employers, managers, or supervisors want to admit that their company could be the site of personal injury or death. Some people mistakenly believe that talking about something leads to a greater risk of its occurring. Moreover, they overlook possible indicators because they have the attitude that, "It's none of my business." Yet safety should be a concern for everyone, especially those persons charged with management and leadership at work.

As we discussed earlier, denial is a typical defense mechanism for warding off anxiety and fear. It is the basic building block of an individual's defense system. This holds true for the psychology of a corporate organization. The subject of violence in the workplace

- Front-line supervisors
- Managers
- Executives
- Human resources personnel
- Health services staff
- Union officials

**Figure 7.2.** Individuals who must be trained.

stirs strong emotions and may engender a response of denial. Sadly, until a violent act actually occurs, some decision makers remain ignorant and unconcerned. Recognizing their organizations' denials, many human resource professionals have asked for advice on broaching this topic and overcoming the denial.

Unquestionably the most salient argument for being proactive is the financial one (see Figure 7.3). *The costs of a traumatic incident can easily exceed a half-million dollars* in lawsuits, property damage, health care and workers' compensation claims, and stress-related injuries and disabilities. Clearly, an ounce of prevention more than equals a pound of cure. Yet the value of preventing a situation that doesn't occur cannot be readily measured. So another useful approach to breaking through denial is the legal one.

*Employers are required by federal and state law to provide a safe workplace*, free from discrimination, harassment, and drugs. A comprehensive program to address hostility and violence meets these minimal standards. Increasingly, companies are being sued and found liable for negligent hiring and failure to intervene with potentially violent employees.

Yet the most appealing argument is how supervisors stand to benefit. *Knowing how to manage potentially hostile employees and about company policies and procedures gives supervisors increased*

---

- Financial costs of workplace hostility and violence
- Federal and state laws
- Benefits to supervisory personnel
- Leadership within industry or geographical area

---

**Figure 7.3.** Justification for training.

*confidence and control.* Their jobs are made easier when they know what to say and do. Ethically they feel *right* about their actions. In turn, their employers gain a better-informed and skilled supervisory group. Further, training supervisors protects employees by lessening the potential for mishandled situations.

It may be helpful to take an informal survey of other companies in a region or industry to see how they are dealing with the matter. This might inspire a company to be a leader in its field, or point out the need to play catch-up. Even if your organization has had no overtly hostile or violent incidents, there may be minor incidents that indicate a potential for more serious events. In approaching decision makers, you should consider which of these arguments—or which combination—is most likely to get and hold management's ear. The goal is to get an acknowledgment of the possibility and seriousness of violence in the workplace.

Once top management has acknowledged the potential, other people in the organization will fall in line. Front-line supervisors absorb what management does, not what it says. So it is essential to establish a supportive attitude before making other interventions. Plan to address attitude during the initial sessions of the training program.

## KNOWLEDGE NEEDED

In chapters 2, 4, and 5 we discussed the warning signs for hostility and violence. In addition to this material, a comprehensive training program should include information on the company's policy statement and procedures, facts about alcohol and drugs, the role of employee assistance personnel or other mental health services, and the basics of effective communication. Although the amount of information is extensive, the primary objective must be simple. The training should answer one question: What must I do as supervisor to ensure a safe workplace for all employees?

Since drug use is highly correlated with hostile and violent behavior, alcohol and drug information is an essential part of management training. In the *Seventh Special Report to U.S. Congress on Alcohol and Health*, the National Institute of Drug Abuse and the National Institute of Mental Health reported the data shown in Figure 7.4 and Tables 7.1 and 7.2.

| | |
|---|---|
| 1. | Alcohol remains the most abused drug in the United States. At least 10% of workers have an alcohol problem. |
| 2. | Marijuana, cocaine, amphetamines and barbiturates are the preferred drugs at work. An estimated 10 million people, 70% of whom are employed, use illegal drugs. |
| 3. | At some point in their lives, 15 million Americans (usually between the ages of 30 and 44) suffer clinical depression, accounting for 88 million lost days of work. |
| 3. | Alcohol is involved in 47% of industrial accidents and 40% of fatalities on the job. |
| 4. | Approximately 56% of drug users engage in illegal activities at work, including drug possession, sale, theft, and prostitution. |
| 5. | In 1993, the cost of substance abuse to U.S. business was $140 billion. |
| 6. | In 1990, depression cost U.S. businesses $44 billion in lost productivity, absenteeism, and health care claims (Neergaard, 1993). |
| 7. | For every $1 invested in employee assistance programs, companies receive a return of at least $4. |

**Figure 7.4.** Facts about alcohol, drugs, and depression.

Supervisors must consider how they can ensure a safe workplace for all employees. This begins with fair and respectful behavior. Again and again research has revealed that those who commit violent acts have a profound feeling of unfairness. The way companies and managers treat people profoundly affects their potential for hostility and violence. Management style delivers a strong message about whether employees are trusted and valued.

## COMMUNICATION SKILLS

Regardless of the best-worded policies, supervisors convey the organization's philosophy by the way they communicate. The typical manager spends over half the workday listening to others, yet most managers learn nothing of this skill in traditional school systems. Instead, the focus is on reading and writing (where manag-

### TABLE 7.1
### Percentage of Employees Using Drugs,
### Listed by Occupation and Drug Type

| Occupation | Any illicit drug | Marijuana | Cocaine |
| --- | --- | --- | --- |
| Construction | 15.2% | 14.3% | 2.7% |
| Finance | 5.2 | 4.3 | 2.7 |
| Manufacturing | 7.2 | 6.3 | 1.4 |
| Personal Service | 14.5 | 13.4 | — |
| Professional | 6.4 | 4.9 | 1.2 |
| Public admin. | 5.8 | 4.7 | — |
| Repair | 14.7 | 13.0 | — |
| Retail Trade | 10.1 | 6.0 | 2.3 |
| Transportation | 6.5 | 5.8 | 3.0 |
| Wholesale Trade | 8.4 | 8.3 | — |

**Note:** A dash (—) indicates percentage is negligible.
**Source:** National Institute of Drug Abuse Household Survey

## TABLE 7.2
## Percentage of 18- to 34-Year-Old Employees Using Drugs, Listed by Occupation and Drug Type

| Occupation | Any illicit drug | Marijuana | Cocaine |
|---|---|---|---|
| Construction | 28.0% | 26.8% | 5.2% |
| Finance | 12.8 | 11.6 | 6.0 |
| Manufacturing | 14.1 | 12.8 | 2.6 |
| Professional | 14.6 | 11.4 | 3.0 |
| Public admin. | 8.0 | 6.9 | 1.7 |
| Repair | 18.7 | 16.3 | 4.0 |
| Retail Trade | 13.2 | 10.2 | 4.2 |
| Personal Service | 20.1 | 19.3 | 3.4 |
| Transportation | 15.2 | 13.7 | 6.3 |
| Wholesale Trade | 20.4 | 20.0 | 4.0 |

**Source:** National Institute of Drug Abuse Household Survey

ers spend less than 10% of their time) and on speaking (where they invest about 33% of their time). If supervisors are to ensure a safe workplace, they must take the time to listen closely to each individual's concerns before doing anything else.

Effective communication begins with learning *active listening*. Too many people assume that, because sounds are passing through their ears, they are "listening." Yet receiving information orally involves more than hearing words. Active listening catches the meaning and the feelings beneath it.

As with any new skill, it takes time and practice to incorporate active listening in the workplace. As all adult learners, supervisors and managers require relevancy and repetition. They must link the issues covered in a training program to their current tasks. If they cannot identify a situation related to the training concepts, they will be unable to use the information. It will be as if they never attended the program. For this reason, organizations should offer training on a yearly basis. Only when learners have unanswered questions are they ready to search for solutions.

## TAKING ACTION

What follows are some guidelines for the front-line supervisor charged with ensuring a safe workplace:

Observe the performance and behavior of all workers every day. Keep written notes in your personal file. If you suspect a problem, contact the employee assistance personnel. If you are certain a problem exists, follow these steps:

1. Identify signs and patterns of job performance.

2. Document what you observe.

    a. Include date, place, who was involved, and what happened.

    b. List negative impacts of each incident.

    Figure 7.5 shows a example of such documentation.

3. Talk to the worker about performance and job standards.

    a. Talk about the performance problem. Point out what you've observed.

    b. Listen to the employee's response.

    c. Identify if anything is keeping the employee from doing the job. Determine if the employee needs additional resources or training. Ask if he or she needs a different management style.

    d. Identify whether you hear acceptance or denial of the problem.

| Date | Incident | Negative Impacts |
|------|----------|------------------|
| **4/2** | | |
| **Reason:** "Car wouldn't start. Heavy traffic." | Late 20 minutes; | Coworkers complained; loss of productivity on shift; spent my time talking with employee and doing the work |
| **4/13** | | |
| **Reason:** "Had the flu. Up all night and finally fell asleep just before shift | Absent; didn't call until 2 hours into shift | Short-handed; overtime costs required to meet production schedule; morale problems; spent half-hour finding replacement |

**Figure 7.5.** A supervisor's documentation.

    e.  Specify the improvements needed. Make sure the employee understands your expectations by asking what he or she has heard and what he or she is going to do differently.

    f.  Encourage the employee by stating your belief that he or she can do it.

4.  Monitor the employee's job performance. Keep track of what happens. Meet regularly until the work has stabilized at an acceptable level.

5.  Follow up promptly

6.  Refer the worker to employee assistance personnel, a psychologist, or a mental health agency.

If the performance problem goes away and then returns, or if it remains unchanged, talk with the employee again. Give the situation a couple more weeks. Continue to observe job performance. If the problem persists, continue along to the next level in the PDP.

# Chapter 8

# EMPLOYEE EDUCATION

Promoting a safe workplace goes hand in hand with educating employees about the organization's mission and philosophy. All employees at every level should share a passion for treating people humanely and a commitment to nonviolent ways of resolving conflict.

## PRESCREENING AND ORIENTATION

During the hiring stage, one must assess several important characteristics of a prospective employee—not only skills, knowledge, and understanding of the job but also personality, work style, values, and attitude. One must determine whether this person has the necessary physical, intellectual, and emotional qualities to do the job successfully and to fit into the workplace. While there is no way to be sure that a person is right for the position until he or she is performing, one can increase the chance of a positive outcome by investing in a thorough orientation program once the person is on the job.

The following is an example of what often happens in the workplace.

A position remains vacant for several months while management goes through the process of selecting the right person. As a result, the immediate supervisor and coworkers are performing without a needed employee. They are working harder, perhaps even putting in extra hours. Workloads are large and backing up. The unit and larger organization are contracted.

Finally, an announcement is posted that the new employee will begin work on Monday. A collective sigh of relief rises from the floor. The supervisor and coworkers anticipate an immediate reduction in their workloads.

But the time frame for learning a new job typically is six months to a year. The new employee will need a great deal of direct instruction and feedback before he or she can function up to standard. Given the expectations of supervisor and coworkers, this is a no-win situation. The new employee will consume resources already in short supply due to the ongoing overload. No wonder many work units make short shrift of the orientation period. They can't afford to educate the new person because they desperately need his or her output as quickly as possible.

Human resource managers know this scenario flirts with failure, both organizationally and individually. If the goals are to increase productivity, add to the bottom line, *and* maintain a safe and humane workplace, we must intervene in the process. This is why educating employees is so important.

## ELEMENTS OF EMPLOYEE EDUCATION

In educating employees about the company's commitment to a humane work environment, you need several elements. Employees must understand the company's policies and procedures on a nonhostile work environment, sexual harassment, and a drug-free workplace. While distributing documents on these topics and posting them on bulletin boards fulfills a company's legal obligations, it fails to communicate the strength of the company's convictions in the way a more direct approach would. Moreover, talking to employees directly creates important connections between management and workers, dissolving the potential of an anonymous workplace.

Since hostility and violence can be provoked by alcohol and other drugs, employee education should contain information about drug use and abuse, including the data shown in Figure 7.4 and Tables 7.1 and 7.2.

Like supervisors, some employees may be reluctant to confront the issue of how to relate respectfully to coworkers. Their denial takes the form of a complaint: "Everyone knows how to treat each other. Why do we need a workshop on this topic?" But in today's diverse workplace, the need to discuss and identify how to relate respectfully takes on new meaning. Words, gestures, facial expressions, and even silence are open to interpretation. Employees cannot assume they know what these common responses mean.

For example, in the traditional cultures of China, Japan, Korea, and Thailand, looking directly into another person's eyes is viewed as disrespectful. So some Asian people have a tendency to avoid eye contact. Even within European cultures, certain kinds of eye contact may be interpreted as threatening. Certainly, between the genders, gestures, eye contact, and body language may take on very different meanings. As the workforce becomes more diversified, employers must educate their workers about these and other issues of respect, dignity, and courtesy.

Employees need information on how to do their jobs and get along with others. And if they notice behavior that is out of the ordinary, they need to know what to do. Many people confront issues on their own; others need the safety and assurance of having the supervisor deal with the matter. The company must indicate those circumstances when an employee can initiate action with the supervisor or other designated representative. The educational program should cover the procedure to follow when an employee brings a concern to management. Who will hear the issue? What other people may become involved? Could the employee experience any repercussions should the matter be judged as lacking in seriousness? What is the company prepared to do to ensure each person's well-being?

## SUMMARY

Any employee education program should cover several points, including these:

- Review the company's policies and procedures

- Explain the reasoning behind the policies

- Define behaviors that are not tolerated in the workplace

- Describe the administrative steps that will be taken if the objectionable behaviors occur

- Allow time for workers to discuss the issues so there is clarity and consensus

- Review the material when there are changes in personnel or policies

Often, companies videotape their group training programs and play them for new hires, in an effort to keep them informed.

As changes occur more and more rapidly in the workplace, employers must ensure that their workers are prepared to meet the challenges of new technology, increased diversity, and organizational differences. Information and communication are essential in improving workers' tolerance for and acceptance of these changes.

# Chapter 9

# EMPLOYEE ASSISTANCE SERVICES

The purpose of an employee assistance program (EAP) is to help workers perform their best by dealing with any personal problems that get in the way of doing their jobs. Better performance translates into greater productivity and larger profits. Thus EAPs are oriented toward supporting management in its efforts to make money. Simultaneously EAPs bring a humane note into the workplace because they are designed to promote the well-being of the workforce. An effective EAP can help management prevent hostility and violence and intervene constructively if it occurs. In addition, in recent years EAP services have grown from purely clinical services for individual employees to consultation services for the organization at large.

## HISTORICAL OVERVIEW

Most people think of an EAP as a counseling resource. Indeed, most EA professionals have expertise in marital and family discord, mental illness, addiction, and codependency. Some programs even provide financial and legal information. Conceived in the early 1970s by the National Institute of Alcohol Abuse and Alcoholism (NIAAA), EAPs are an outgrowth of the company employee alcohol programs begun in the late 1930s and 1940s. Alcoholics Anonymous (AA) showed families and employers that "hopelessly drunk" people could successfully recover from the ravages of alcoholism and resume their roles as responsible and contributing members of society. So delighted by this actuality were large organizations that they readily agreed to have some of their workers do outreach among other employees still afflicted. Initially the efforts consisted of practicing AA's 12th step, "carrying the message to those who still suffer." From these informal efforts evolved more structured programs, such as holding AA meetings on company grounds. Despite variations in how company programs were organized, the principal remained unchanged: One recovering person helps another.

Employee alcohol programs worked. They provided employers with many unforeseen benefits. Besides rehabilitating employees who had ceased being productive, they also reduced absenteeism, turnover, health care costs, and morale problems. When the Hughes Act established the National Institute of Alcohol Abuse and Alcoholism (NIAAA), it expanded this concept while overcoming the stigma associated with employee alcohol programs.

Since the early stages of alcoholism negatively affect family life, finances, and health, employers could detect alcohol abusers and intervene before individuals and their families were decimated by full-blown alcoholism, broadening company programs to include any kind of personal difficulty. And so the idea of employee assistance was born.

NIAAA further promoted the idea of employee assistance by funding and training two outreach workers for each state, one each focusing on public and private organizations. By providing free technical assistance, the Galloping 100, as they were called, encouraged employers to establish EAPs. NIAAA also funded graduate programs in social work and psychology, turning out more people to populate EAPs. It created a profession.

Not long after, external EAP providers appeared, followed by the Association of Labor, Management, and Consultants in Alcoholism (ALMACA), now known as the Employee Assistance Professional Association (EAPA). More recently another trade organization has emerged—the Employee Assistance Society of North America (EASNA)—whose focus is on the United States and Canada. In less than 20 years, with the publication of a newsletter, trade journal, and certification of workers and programs, an industry has grown from the ravages of alcoholism—one dedicated to health care and wellness in the workplace.

Today many municipal and private organizations have EAPs. Generally the broad range of activities include policy development; management training; employee education; clinical interventions, including assessment, referral, counseling, follow-up, and case management; and management consultation. Some EAPs also offer critical incident debriefings, preemployment screenings, and fitness-for-duty evaluations. If an organization is committed to preventing hostility in the workplace, an EAP is a vital resource. The EA professional can support efforts to ensure a safe workplace.

## POLICY DEVELOPMENT

In chapter 6, we discussed the value of having certain policies in place. Organizations need policies outlawing any form of hostility and violence, including racial and sexual harassment, and any use of alcohol or illegal drugs. Policies not only provide a framework for the company's legal obligation to maintain a safe and drug-free environment that protects the rights of all workers, they also outline procedures for addressing and rectifying problems that affect this commitment.

An employee assistance program can help a company establish policies. In some cases it will have sample policies that can be modify for the specific business situation. If your company is developing such policies, you should have the EA professional review it and identify the program's specific role. If company policies are already written, make sure your EA staff has a copy, so they know the company's orientation and expectations.

For example, in designing a policy on harassment, one organization determined that anyone who alleges or is accused of harassment will be referred to the EAP for stress management services. Another company refers employees who test positive for drugs to its EAP for an assessment and treatment recommendations. Yet a third enterprise uses its EAP to conduct fitness-for-duty evaluations and make recommendations to the medical department. Many EA professionals can provide all these services and more.

*Typically, a company should avoid having its EAP associated with any investigation or disciplinary action.* The EA staff should remain neutral and be seen as a resource to help employees and supervisors cope with stressful situations. This neutrality in no way negates their ability to consult with management in determining a strategy for resolving employee complaints. It simply positions the EAP as a source of professional consultation and advocacy for those who seek it.

## MANAGEMENT TRAINING

EA professionals conduct annual workshops to train supervisors, managers, human resources agents, medical staff, and even union representatives on how to identify and intervene with "troubled employees"—those whose job performance has been negatively affected by personal problems. Hostile and potentially violent workers are a subset of troubled employees. Thus, the same training can be modified to detect signs of workplace violence.

In chapter 7 we discussed the content of a management training program that addresses hostility and violence in the workplace. Most EA professionals have the knowledge and skill to organize and present such workshops. Their understanding of how to identify a troubled employee and how to intervene successfully forms the basis of this training. Moreover, they have expertise in communication skills, an essential ingredient for preventing the escalation of violence. Since supervisors should refer all suspected or actual hostile employees for assessment and counseling, the EAP is an excellent choice for conducting or facilitating this training.

## EMPLOYEE EDUCATION

The EAP generally provides educational sessions for employees as part of its overall services. Usually the information emphasizes wellness issues. By way of introduction, EA professionals cover a variety of topics, from parenting and communication to personal growth, substance abuse, and finances.

Just as they can modify their training for supervisors, EA professionals can educate employees about violence at work. All people in the workplace should know the signs of hostile workers and what their organization expects them to do if they suspect, witness, or are victims of hostility and violence. They must become familiar with the company's policies and procedures.

Employees usually are the first to detect when something's wrong. Their observations are invaluable in identifying at an early stage those people who are at-risk for hostile and violent behavior. Unless they know what actions to take, however, their knowledge and suspicions are lost to the organization. Employees need to learn what to notice and what to do, especially when the situation is urgent. These action steps should be outlined clearly in the company's policy statement. (See chapter 6 for a sample policy.)

Employee education should cover three types of threats:

- those from fellow employees,

- those from outside suppliers and customers, and

- those from domestic partners.

Workers should be assured that their safety and well-being matter, and that their employer is prepared to take the necessary actions to protect them. Most importantly, *the message should be loud and clear that the company will not tolerate any threatened or actual hostility or violence.*

The EAP's presence communicates that there are resources available should employees suspect or experience hostility and violence. It provides each employee a confidential setting to talk about these issues and get help.

## CLINICAL INTERVENTIONS

The main expertise EA professionals bring to the workplace is an ability to conduct assessments and make referrals to community treatment resources. Most clinical staff members are trained in one of the helping professions: social work, psychology, marriage and family counseling, psychiatric nursing, drug and alcohol counseling, or pastoral counseling. They are experienced in interviewing clients and determining their sources of distress rapidly. Furthermore, because they understand how personal problems affect work performance, they can recommend specific interventions that will bring immediate improvement. For example, by referring an employee to needed child-care resources, an EA counselor enables the woman to extend her work hours so that she can attend a weekly planning session. Another worker might be helped to learn computer skills when he is diagnosed with a hearing loss and referred for treatment.

EA professionals typically compile an extensive list of community agencies and private practitioners who provide a range of services, from alcohol and drug treatment to financial counseling. Because of variations in health plans, they keep information on insurance eligibility, office locations and hours, handicapped access, fluency in foreign languages, and qualifications and expertise of individual staff members. In matching clients to service providers, EA counselors also rely on "chemistry"—their ability to assess style and personality. Thus the referral aspect of an EA practice is both a science and an art, knowledge of both needs and preferences.

After the assessment and referral, EA clinicians continue to follow the client to determine whether the treatment plan and referral sources are helpful, and to what extent the personal problems are being resolved. When the client reports difficulties on the job, the professional also collects information on the individual's work performance from the client and, with permission, from the supervisor. During this phase of case management, the individual may have periodic contact with the EA counselor. Clients always have the option of returning to the EA worker for additional services for the same or different matters.

People access the EAP's clinical services in two ways:

1. they can initiate help on their own, or

2. they can be directed to the EAP by their supervisor, manager, union representative, or human resources staff.

While individuals usually are more motivated when they come on their own steam, being referred can be beneficial—as long as the referring agent informs the EA professional about the exact nature of the referral. (See Figure 9.1 for an outline of a supervisor's referral form.) In either case, the EA counselor conducts a thorough assessment as outlined above.

If an employee is directed to the EAP, the referring agent provides concrete facts about the employee's behavior. The EA professional must know what the worker was like in the past.

How did he or she perform?

How did he or she get along with coworkers?

How has the person been evaluated?

The clinician also needs information about recent behavior.

What did the employee do that prompted the referral?

Have there been any changes in work or supervisory assignments?

**Figure 9.1.** Outline of supervisory referral intake form.

Referring agent's name & title:_____

Telephone number:_____

Department:_____

Employee's name:_____

Position:_____

Job responsibilities:_____

_____

_____

Number of years with company:_____

Number of years in position:_____

Past evaluation(s):_____

_____

_____

Current job performance problem:_____

_____

_____

Past job performance problems:_____

_____

_____

_____

Management actions taken to date:_____

_____

_____

_____

Disciplinary status of employee:_____

_____

_____

**Figure 9.1.** Continued.

Personal information about employee:_____

_____

_____

_____

Relevant information about company or department:_____

_____

_____

_____

EAP recommendation:_____

_____

_____

_____

_____

Are there any personal circumstances that might be affecting the employee?

At the same time, the EA professional asks about management's response to the employee's behavior.

How many times has the supervisor discussed the situation with the employee?

What were the results?

Have any disciplinary measures been applied?

Is the employee in jeopardy of losing his or her job?

This knowledge enables the EA clinician to identify discrepancies between the client's and the supervisor's perceptions of the problem, so he or she can make an informed decision when recommending an intervention.

How do the EAPs address workplace violence? Employees who are suspected of hostility or who are clearly hostile meet one-to-one with an EA professional. Clinicians are sanctioned to raise questions that supervisors, managers, and even human resources staff cannot or should not ask. Also, EA staff can conduct psychological evaluations (see chapter 3). The knowledge gained this way helps the organization determine how to proceed with the employee in a fair and humane way. Moreover, the process demonstrates to coworkers and the union that management is serious about ensuring a safe workplace for everyone.

If the EA professional finds that the employee lacks skills in handling and discharging anger, he or she may refer the individual to a psychoeducational program, stress management workshop, or exercise program. Short-term or extended counseling may alter the individual's attitude, thought processes, and behavior. Medication may be effective in reducing angry thoughts and increasing temper control. Simply getting attention from the EA professional may help the employee regain perspective and eliminate feelings of despair and hopelessness.

## MANAGEMENT CONSULTATION

Having worked with a variety of organizations, supervisors, and employees, EA professionals understand workplace dynamics. Generally, they know how people respond to different types of management styles and can anticipate likely consequences. This enables them to advise management on how to handle numerous situations and mitigate the negative affects on workers.

Supervisors, managers, union representatives, medical staff, and human resources staff can consult the EAP when employees are performing poorly on the job or are behaving oddly in the workplace. While discouraged from diagnosing personal problems, the EA professional can educate managers on how behavioral-medical problems are manifested at work. (See chapter 4 for a more detailed discussion of warning signs.)

Over the course of a calendar year, nearly 25% of the workforce could be classified as "troubled employees," yet most supervisors lack experience in handling this matter. Consequently, they appreciate support and guidance when faced with such a problem. With the human resources department often understaffed and overworked, the EAP provides a vital source of help to individual supervisors. Moreover, since the service is confidential, some supervisors prefer to raise their concerns with the EAP because they know their privacy will be respected.

Typically, EA professionals set the stage for management consultation during supervisory training sessions. Besides educating attendees about signs of a troubled employee, EA staff emphasize their availability to consult with supervisors on many topics, including:

identifying a troubled employee;

informing his or her manager, union, and human resources;

planning the initial confrontation;

making the initial referral to EAP;

intervening with the individual on an ongoing basis; and

applying disciplinary measures, including termination, if necessary.

EA staff also can consult with supervisors about individual employees; two or more workers in conflict; traumatic episodes in the work unit, department, or organization; and anticipated changes such as layoffs. Once the supervisor initiates the consultation, the EA professional continues to monitor events and offer advice. Often he or she participates in sessions with the supervisor, manager, union representative, and human resources personnel to plan strategies for approaching a troubled employee. Orchestrating the actions of all key players greatly increases the likelihood that the employee gets help.

Although EA practitioners do not provide legal advice, their familiarity with labor laws, discrimination, disability, and harassment issues gives companies an extra edge in treating employees fairly and humanely. Since fairness is such a crucial concern to the potentially violent employee, and because the EAP often is external to the organization, EA professionals are essential to maintaining safe workplaces, especially when emotions and frustration are running high.

## CRISIS INTERVENTION

In the following sections on crisis intervention, preemployment screenings, and at-risk evaluations, please note that not every EAP provides them or is capable of doing so. Usually in-house EA practitioners lack the expertise to conduct psychological testing, as this work requires specific training and certification dramatically different from that needed to provide other EAP services.

Despite a company's best intentions, traumatic and violent events may occur. Because of their experience working with people who are upset and consulting with management on difficult personnel situations, EA professionals are excellent resources for responding to a workplace crisis. (Chapter 11 covers this topic in more detail.)

Prior to a crisis, EA professionals can help the organization develop plans for how it will respond. At the time of the crisis, they consult with management on staging debriefing programs. They conduct debriefings for the management group, those individuals immediately involved, other employees, and family members where appropriate. EA practitioners also are available for individual and family counseling. Of course, they continue to provide management consultation and assessment and referrals for troubled employees. Months later, the EA professionals meet with those people who attended debriefings to monitor their recovery. Together these services constitute the basics of a comprehensive crisis intervention.

## PREEMPLOYMENT SCREENING

In chapter 6 we discussed ways to avoid hiring potentially violent employees. One of these ways was screening applicants psychologically to rule out overtly violent people prior to making a job offer. Some EA professionals can provide preemployment screens. Sometimes, these screenings will be provided by outside consultants.

## AT-RISK ASSESSMENT

In any given business employing human beings, a small percentage of the workforce will at some time report for work in a condition that raises concerns about their ability to perform safely on the job. If a supervisor suspects that an employee is impaired physically or psychologically, the employee should be relieved of any immediate duties and evaluated. Failure to act could lead to a variety of negative consequences, including accidents, equipment failures, injuries, violent behavior, and loss of life. Not only are these possibilities costly, they also may increase the organization's legal liability.

Depending on the individual's behavior, a fitness-for-duty evaluation should be conducted by a psychologist, psychiatrist, or medical doctor. Most EAPs either have on staff or can recommend licensed psychologists who can perform such evaluations. Management should consult the EA professional to determine what actions to take for any given situation, including a psychological evaluation of the individual's mental status, drug and alcohol use, and aggressiveness. (See chapter 3 for more details.)

# Chapter 10

# SECURITY TECHNOLOGY AND PERSONAL SAFETY

*By Michael G. McCourt[1]*

*If you fail to plan, you can plan to fail.*

As we have seen, a systemic approach to managing workplace hostility and violence is crucial for success. Policies, training, and planning are all important elements of your response protocol.

---

[1] Michael McCourt is president of MGM Associates Inc., a Massachusetts-based consulting firm specializing in employee and management development. With more than 20 years' experience in law enforcement, MGM Associates Inc. provides consultation and training in critical incident stress, workplace violence, and risk management.

Michael also is Director of Risk Management for American Properties Team Inc., a real estate management company with properties in three states. As a national and international trainer and guest speaker, he has provided service to a diverse cross-section of industries, including transportation, communication, manufacturing, high tech, and managed health care.

Michael received his Bachelor of Science degree in Criminal Justice and holds a Master of Arts degree in Public Administration. He is a member of the American Society of Industrial Security.

There are two other important elements of a systemic approach to workplace violence, and they are often overlooked by organizations:

1. *security technology* (or hardware) and

2. *personal safety initiatives.*

Companies typically are reluctant to address these issues, approaching them with an attitude that seems to say, "If you build it, they will come." But the goal of providing security is not to turn companies into virtual prisons; an organization's response to violence should be in direct proportion to its greatest potential threat. We've all heard the saying, "Let the punishment fit the crime." In the case of preventing workplace violence, *let the technology fit the threat*. The goal of addressing workplace violence should be a reasonable, balanced, strategic, and functional response to unusual workplace incidents.

The same can be said for developing safety protocols and training programs aimed at teaching personal safety measures. Our society has adopted a passive attitude toward personal safety. We seem to throw up our hands and say, "It's someone else's responsibility to protect me." Personal safety and the liability associated with it are placed at the feet of the government (both federal and state) and of the employer. Yet, while it's true that employers must make a good faith effort to provide safe work environments for their employees, the ultimate responsibility for personal safety remains with the individual.

No one yet has defined what constitutes a "good faith effort." Does it involve a floor or a ceiling, a security door or a 10-foot wall? How much is enough? What is overkill? What constitutes negligent security? These are challenging questions for the employers of the 1990s and beyond. And while there are no hard and fast rules, there are some sensible guidelines employers can follow to help avert and to develop an appropriate response to potential violence.

## ASSESSING YOUR POTENTIAL FOR VIOLENCE

*An ounce of prevention is worth a pound of cure.*

Most people would agree that spending thousands of dollars in security equipment to protect a corner lemonade stand would be a prime example of overkill. On the other hand, spending several million dollars to protect the Pentagon does not seem unreasonable. Why are we capable of making these distinctions in our minds? What justifies the inequity in expense?

The answer, of course, is relatively simple. The Pentagon houses important information, some dealing with issues of national security. Breaching the security at the Pentagon represents a serious threat to public safety and our national well-being.

On the other hand, the individual operating the corner lemonade stand has invested minimal resources and has little to lose, other than some water, sugar, lemons, and cups. Investing any amount of money in a security system simply is not justified. How, then, do organizations determine budgets and justify investing in security technology? The following items will provide some guidance.

There are several factors to consider in assessing your organization's potential for violence:

- Industry

- Geographic location

- Hours of operations

- Public access

- Past incident

- Current resources

Keep in mind that these are not intended to be all-inclusive. They do, however, provide a sound basis from which companies can determine the approximate cost and complexity of the security resources required for their organizations.

## Industry

In a training session on workplace violence, participants were asked to identify the most violent industry in this country. You probably won't be surprised to hear that the most common response was the U.S. Postal Service. You may be surprised to hear that this answer is incorrect. The Postal Service has inherited a negative reputation that is both unwarranted and undeserved—but that's a story for another time. You might be very surprised to hear that more violence occurs within the health care industry than in any other. (Violence means pushing, shoving, biting, simple assaults, threats, and so on. The emphasis here is not on felonious or fatal assaults.)

It is essential for employers to have a conversational knowledge of the *types* of incidents occurring within their industry, as well as the *frequency* with which they occur. These two elements support the theory of *past incident*, the basis on which many legal decisions are made.

This theory says that companies should be able to predict the future, based on the past. For example, if you are the owner of a convenience store (commonly recognized as high-priority targets for holdups) and you do nothing to protect your employees from being robbed, you could be found liable for negligent security if one of your employees is hurt in a robbery. While that may not seem fair, it's an emerging trend in our legal system and an important concept for employers to understand. Essentially, the courts are asking employers to predict and plan for future events.

Bleak as that may seem, there is hope. Remember that employers are held to the standard of making a "good faith effort," and that has yet to be defined. The idea is to take *reasonable* precautions based on past incidents in your industry. With a little research, employers can determine the level of risk commonly associated with their field. There are a number of organizations in both the public and private sectors that can provide reports on violence within industries.

Once the level of violent activity has been determined, building a systemic response equal to or slightly greater than that level will go a long way toward building a defense against litigation. The key is research and planning.

## Geographic Location

Violence typically requires three elements: a host, a setting, and a permissive attitude. The environment in which you operate is another key element in protecting your employees.

A number of variables affect your geographic environment: income levels, education levels, ethnicity, population, physical access, neighboring industry, public safety resources, and rural or urban settings are but a few of the factors to take into account when assessing your environment.

The local police are your best resource for assessing your environment. Most police departments have an officer assigned to act as liaison with the business community. These officers are trained in crime prevention and are familiar with corporate needs. Developing a working relationship with them, *prior to an incident,* is crucial. Should an incident result in litigation, any attorney worth his or her salt will visit the local police to determine whether you have established a relationship with them. The police department also can give you reports of crime in your area, which you can use to develop an appropriate security response.

It is also important to know what your competitors are doing to address violence. This is another area that will be examined in cases involving litigation. There's a theory in real estate that says you probably don't want to own the worst house on the street or the best house on the street. A property somewhere in the middle, or slightly above, is preferable. The same can be said for security systems. Make sure you're not the proud owner of the worst security program in the neighborhood.

## Hours of Operation

Historically, organizations with unusual business hours have been obvious targets for violence and criminal activity. Individuals prone to violent or criminal behavior operate best under certain conditions: low or limited lighting and environments with few or no witnesses. Businesses with 24-hour operations or second and third shifts, therefore, are prime targets for crime. Examples are obvious: convenience stores, liquor stores, manufacturing plants, hospitals, and fast-food chains are some targeted industries.

If your business requires unusual hours of operation, there are some simple steps you can take to limit your exposure to violence:

- Increase lighting in the area.

- Keep windows clear of signs and displays, providing a better view for passing patrols.

- Use a drop safe to avoid having large amounts of cash on hand.

- Establish a working relationship with the local police, and encourage frequent patrols.

- If possible, have at least two employees on duty at all times.

- When appropriate, use alarms and closed-circuit television (CCTV) systems.

- Establish a periodic call-in schedule, to ensure the safety of your employees.

No strategy is foolproof, but these simple steps can reduce your risk of becoming the next victim of violence.

**Public Access**

Depending on which surveys you read, workplace homicide is now the number one cause of death for women, and the number three cause of death for men. The surveys, however, don't tell the entire story. What they omit is the fact that most fatal attacks in the workplace are at the hands of third parties; *they are not precipitated by fellow employees.* For that reason, public access is an important consideration.

Organizations fall into one of two categories: those with restricted access and those with open access. Those with open access present the most significant security challenge.

Examples of open-access organizations are hospitals, banks, retail stores, and restaurants—in short, most public-sector operations. These organizations are referred to as *open* because they invite the general public in for business. Restricting access would be counterproductive to their existence, yet it's their accessibility that makes them so vulnerable.

Private companies that can restrict access to employees and those conducting valid business, can use identification cards, electronic or computerized card access systems, closed-circuit television monitoring, and private security guards.

Employers should identify their client base, assess the nature of their business, and carefully consider its dependence on public access. If the success of their business depends on public access, the security tips listed under hours of operations apply.

**Past Incident**

We talked about the theory of past incident above. But there are other important points to keep in mind when reviewing past incidents.

It is important for employers to keep track of the kinds of incidents occurring within their organization and their industry. Tracking these incidents can help you determine your strategy for preventing future incidents.

For example, suppose you are in the banking industry and several customers have been assaulted and robbed at local ATM machines. Your strategy for preventing future robberies might include increasing lighting, using CCTV equipment, enclosing the ATM inside the foyer of your bank, or improving visibility for passing patrols. The options you choose would depend on the type of activity occurring at that particular ATM location.

Two other important factors are the frequency with which incidents occur and the date of the last incident. If you experienced two incidents, five years apart, and the last one occurred six years ago, your strategy would be quite different than if you had experienced several incidents within the last few months.

Employers should keep track of incident reports and review them periodically. Identifying trends and developing an appropriate response will reduce your exposure to liability, should an incident occur.

## Current Resources

The last factor in assessing potential for violence is your current resources. This refers to the technology already installed within a business, or those procedures now being used to protect the organization. Common examples include closed-circuit television monitoring systems, alarm systems, and card access systems.

For the smaller organization, investing in sophisticated technology may be out of the question. Upgrading technology might range from increasing lighting to installing a CCTV unit.

On the other hand, larger organizations in high-risk industries may want to develop a capital budget for a more sophisticated security system. The choice of a would be based on all of the factors discussed above. For the most part, the only thing an organization can do wrong is to do nothing at all.

# CHOOSING THE APPROPRIATE TECHNOLOGY

*Remember, the life you save may be your own.*
—Smokey the Bear

Having assessed your risk potential for violence, the next step is selecting the *appropriate* security technology, based on your industry and organizational needs. Technology ranges from the very simple (personal alarms worn by the employee) to the very sophisticated (voice exemplar systems). The key is choosing technology that will increase current levels of safety without breaking the bank. Neither end of the spectrum will serve for the average company. Therefore, we will limit our discussion to the most commonly used systems in the public and private sectors: closed-circuit television monitoring cameras (CCTV), audible or silent alarm systems, and card access systems.

## Closed-Circuit Television Monitoring Systems (CCTV)

CCTV technology has been around for many years, although current systems are far superior to their predecessors in both picture quality and function. Prices range from several hundred to several thousand dollars. The difference in price is based primarily on function and the quality of the image required. Selecting the proper system can be tricky, and this is an area where a professional consultant can be of great assistance.

Surveillance systems can be overt or covert, depending on their purpose. *Overt systems* (easily seen or detected) are used primarily to prevent or deter incidents from occurring. *Covert systems* are used to catch someone in the act of doing something illegal or contrary to the good of the organization. Be careful to check local laws regarding privacy before you install a covert system. Surveillance of common areas (where there is no "expectation of privacy") is almost always legal. Common areas include parking lots, entryways, hallways, reception areas, stairwells, and public areas.

Electronic surveillance is one of the most effective ways to deter criminal activity. Once installed, a good system will last for years, making it a sound investment.

## Alarm Systems

One of the most common security devices used by corporations and homeowners alike is the electronic alarm system. Again, there is a wide variety of types and models from which to choose. The cost and complexity of a system should be directly proportionate to the property or product being protected.

Some basic features distinguish alarm systems:

They may be audible or silent.

They may sound in a central receiving station or go directly to the local police.

They may include perimeter protection and motion detectors.

They may contain remote back-up transmitters.

They may or may not have reset devices.

When you are buying an alarm system, hiring a professional consultant can save you money and headaches in the long run.

Alarm systems can be triggered in a number of ways. In the case of workplace violence, it's important to include strategically placed panic buttons, capable of immediately activating the alarm. Seconds count when someone is being assaulted, and the sound of a screaming alarm could provide your employees the time they need to escape.

Triggering an alarm sends a signal to one of two places: a central alarm station or the local police. Central alarm stations monitor several alarm systems and notify the police after receiving an alarm. These stations typically function very well. The only disadvantage to using an alarm station is building in a second step in the response process. Once the alarm has been triggered, the signal must be received and the address identified. In most cases, a call is then placed to verify the need for response, and only then is a call placed to the local police. On a busy night, there can be a significant delay between the time the signal is received and time the police are contacted. This reinforces the utility of an audible alarm.

Unfortunately, a central alarm system often is the only option available. Many police departments will no longer accept a direct alarm, due to a reduction in human resources. Check with your local police department before selecting an alarm system.

Systems can protect the perimeter of the building, and often the interior portions of the building, through the use of motion detectors. The key to protecting the perimeter is to include *every accessible door and window*. Any breach in the system weakens the overall level of protection. Basement and first-floor doors and windows should always be included, as well as any second- or third-floor doors and windows accessible from fire escapes or roof-tops. Protection of higher levels of a building usually is afforded by comprehensive coverage of lower floors.

Alarm systems operate on electrical current and, therefore, are susceptible to power failures and criminal intervention. Make sure to include a remote transmitter when selecting a system. This will guard against power failures and outside tampering.

## Card Access

The new kid on the security block is card access. Most people have already experienced this technology in the form of their local ATM machine. Inserting a bank card into a slot provides access to the automated teller. The same concept is applied in business to provide employees access to restricted buildings and areas.

For the most part, card access is available in two flavors: card swipe (similar to readers in gas stations) and proximity card readers. Proximity cards, as the name implies, allow a person to wave a thin card or fob in front of a reader and gain access to that door.

Card access provides a number of advantages:

First it generates a computerized report of who is accessing the door and when the door is being accessed. This is accomplished by assigning each card holder a coded number. When an individual uses his or her card, a computer records the day, date, time, door, and user requesting access. This is especially useful in investigating larcenies.

Second, it allows the organization to transfer or terminate employees without having to rekey the entire building. The coded number assigned to that employee is simply removed from the system. This simplifies replacing lost keys as well.

Finally, card access allows employers to provide access to individual doors within an organization, based on actual need. This eliminates concerns over the use of master keys.

Systems are not as expensive as you might think. This technology is now being used to protect employees and property across a diverse cross-section of industries.

There are many other types of systems available. Some are very progressive but relatively untested. Some have established track records but are very expensive. Your system should be tailored to the needs of your organization.

Some simple guidelines apply when purchasing security technology:

Make sure the installer is reputable; ask for references.

Make sure the individual or company is licensed if the installation requires wiring.

Ask about insurance bonds, warranties, and service contracts. Reputable dealers are happy to provide such information.

Remember, technology is only one element of a well-planned and comprehensive approach to workplace violence. It provides one layer in the effort to harden targets against this unusual challenge.

## PERSONAL SAFETY TIPS

### Awareness Is Our Game

If you had taken a survey in the early 1990s and asked the general public to name the number one problem facing the country, the answer probably would have been illegal drugs. Today, the answer is crime. Things have changed.

People in every community are feeling less safe than in the past. This growing concern with personal safety has created a cottage industry for karate schools across the country. Corporations are inviting guest speakers to talk about personal safety. In short, people are trying to feel more comfortable with their environment.

Ask any martial artist worth his or her salt, and he or she will tell you that personal safety has more to do with awareness than technical proficiency. Planning and personal awareness can greatly reduce your potential for becoming the victim of crime. Here are some simple guidelines to increase your level of preparedness.

**Toto, I Don't Think We're in Kansas Anymore.**　We live in a violent society. Pick up any newspaper or listen to any newscast, and the first 10 minutes will consist of a collage of human atrocities. Accepting that it can happen in your community, your place of business, or your school district will help you to mentally prepare for the unexpected.

**Go Ahead, Make My Day.**　Many victims *act* like victims. Assailants are adept at identifying submissive postures and behaviors. Walking with confidence, making eye contact, and believing that you are alert and capable of moving within your environment creates a sense of control that assailants are less likely to challenge.

**You Can Run, But You Can't Hide.**　Paying attention to what's often considered the mundane can increase your level of safety. Noticing remote areas on your commute to work, studying the layout of your parking facility, thinking of what the area will look like under cover of darkness, and making mental note of the closest phone are some examples of increasing awareness of your personal environment.

**You're in My Space.**    We all exist within two imaginary circles that surround us. One is referred to as our *personal zone*, the other as our *safety zone*.

Our personal zone usually extends seven to eight feet beyond our bodies. This is the area in which our social interaction takes place. We usually invite people into this area for hugs or handshakes. It's also a comfortable zone for conducting conversations, both business and personal.

Our safety zone extends three to four feet beyond our bodies and acts as an invisible protective "bubble." Only a chosen few are allowed into our safety zone, usually people who have earned our trust over time. Safety zones can extend a little further to the rear, given that most of us feel uncomfortable not seeing what's happening behind us. Have you ever been walking down a lonely street at night and heard or sensed someone closing the distance behind you? If so, you have experienced the uncomfortable feeling of knowing that your safety zone is about to be entered.

The key is to be aware of anyone closing distance. (This is an important concept in the martial arts). If you feel uncomfortable with the proximity of an individual, tell him or her to please respect your safety zone.

## The Eyes Have It

There's a theory in our society that says, "The eyes are the mirror of the soul." True or not, there is a great deal to be learned by looking into someone's eyes; not the least of which is their fear factor. Assailants count on this and are quite adept at reading fear.

A strong, confident posture accompanied by direct eye contact can mean the difference between being a victim and being a survivor. Don't confuse this with glaring or exchanging a visual challenge. An appropriate glance says, "I see you there, and I'm not afraid of you," then goes on with business. Two things are accomplished: First, you have sent a message of confidence; second, you have made observations about the individual that will be helpful should the situation deteriorate. *Don't underestimate the power of eye contact.*

### Don't Fence Me In

One of the basic rules of self-defense is this: Don't put yourself in a position from which there is no retreat. Police officers often are accused of sitting with their backs to the wall, even when off-duty. The rationale for this behavior is that it lets them observe movement throughout a room without having to worry about an attack from behind. Often overlooked is the fact that this position provides no immediate means of escape. The theory may work if one is armed, but it has limited application in the workplace.

Try to position yourself in a way that provides options should an incident occur. When driving, leave at least a car's length between you and the vehicle in front of you. Carjackings are on the rise, and this simple measure will provide the opportunity to take evasive action if you are faced with one.

The same concept applies to your office. Try to position yourself so that you have direct access to an exit. When confronting an angry employee, make sure that you factor in an escape route. In addition, make sure you have another employee with you. The old saying is true: There *is* safety in numbers.

When possible, allow space to maneuver in parking lots. If necessary, take the time to back your vehicle into a space. These simple precautions can make a significant difference in a violent situation.

### Read My Lips

We all are familiar with this statement, but it represents only part of the puzzle. To increase your level of safety, you have to read other body language as well. Intense eye contact, closing personal space, a change in skin color, distention of the veins on the head and neck, an increase of volume (or, conversely, total silence), abusive language, threats (direct or indirect), and aggressive or improper physical touching are all signs of potential violence.

Some of these signs are more subtle than others, but everyone displays some change in body language just prior to aggressive behavior. Being able to recognize a change in an employee's normal behavior is the first step in avoiding violence. It is important for employers to be familiar with the baseline behavioral patterns of those who work for them.

Notice that nothing has been discussed here regarding defensive tactics; nor has there been any discussion of responding in an aggressive manner. There are a number of different schools of thought about training employees in self-defense. The decision to resist, if attacked, rests with the individual and is based on variables too numerous to discuss here. In general, most experts agree that avoiding the confrontation always is the preferred option. Common sense, anticipating your environment, and a little vigilance can go a long way toward accomplishing that goal.

## SUMMARY

In this chapter, we've looked at three elements of workplace security: assessing your potential, security technology, and personal safety tips. But we have only scratched the surface here. Every situation is different and calls for a thought-out, tailored response. Organizations sometimes assume that a program that's not expensive or complicated is not effective. This simply is not true. In many cases, paying attention to the basics is all it takes to harden the target and avoid a violent situation.

# Chapter 11

# CRISIS RESPONSE TEAMS

A *crisis* can be defined as a disruption of the normal state of functioning that results in turmoil, instability, and upheaval in a system. The term has received a lot of attention in recent years; we seem to assume that, if we are living our lives "correctly," we should be able to avoid crises. In actuality, humans deal with crises on a daily basis: The car won't start, a snowstorm closes the roads, we lose heat or electricity, we injure ourselves skiing, one of the kids gets sick, we get food poisoning—the list goes on and on.

A more productive way of thinking about a crisis is as an unplanned change that forces the system to make immediate and often long-term accommodations. For most of us, "a disruption of the normal state of functioning that results in turmoil, instability, and upheaval in a system" has become a regular part of our day-to-day activity. Most adults are adept at thinking on their feet in order to manage new situations that are presented by unplanned and unwanted changes. This is true in the workplace, as well. In the last few decades, our workforce has evolved from manufacturing to servicing, which represents a move from assembly-line consistency to the ever-changing needs of clients. From consistency to crisis on a daily basis.

Further, the workplace is a fragile institution, easily affected by politics, financial influences, competition, personnel changes, rumors, labor-management negotiations, and a myriad of other events. Managing change and crises is the name of the game.

Certainly, workplace hostility and violence qualify as crises in any occupational environment. Whether it is an acute incident that starts abruptly and ends traumatically (for example, a physical assault) or a chronic form of hostility (such as sexual harassment), violence and hostility constitute crises—the kinds of crises most of us are unaccustomed to managing. Personal assault, emotional harassment, injury, and destruction of property represent a different type of unplanned change and systemic turmoil; they may leave the workplace reeling for a long time.

As this book has suggested, there are ways we can help:

> We must not overreact and turn the workplace into an armed camp.

> We must have policies, procedures, and programs in place to respond to such an event, should it occur.

> All employees should receive education and training with respect to such policies.

> Each organization should have a crisis response team made up of people from different areas within the workplace, including human resources, EAP, labor, management, occupational health, legal, safety/security, and an outside liaison to community resources. This team should have four goals:

> > 1.  to help establish policy;
> >
> > 2.  to conduct training programs;
> >
> > 3.  to respond to incidents in the workplace; and
> >
> > 4.  to be the eyes and ears of the organization.

Within the team are two groups: one administrative and the other facilitative.

Team members should have clear guidelines on what is expected of them should a crisis occur.

The roles of the team and its members can be seen clearly defined in the following case study:

At work one day, one male employee attacked another. The event was witnessed by several others, who tried to intervene.

The victim was taken to the hospital by one of the workers. The attacker left the workplace before the police arrived. He was later arrested at his home.

The incident had a disruptive effect on the workplace. Coworkers knew both parties, witnessed the incident, were involved with the police and security investigation, and worried about what would happen when the individuals returned to work. Workers were angry with management because the attacker had been difficult to deal with for some time and nothing had been done.

The crisis response team was activated and responded in the following manner:

Human resources, legal, and security members worked as the administrative group, gathering information about the event, communicating with police, and notifying the families of the two workers. They also dealt with issues of disability and insurance coverage. Later, they were involved in investigation and disciplinary actions.

One team member was designated as the media liaison to handle questions from the press about the incident.

The EAP staff, occupational nurse, labor representatives, and management personnel comprised the facilitating component of the team. They talked to the other workers, provided information about the incident, and conducted debriefings. They met with the employees who had witnessed the altercation separately, then held a larger meeting for others in the company. The reasons for the all-personnel meeting were:

1.  to allow workers to discuss their reactions to the incident,

2.  to limit the rumor mill and prevent distortions and misinformation,

3.  to review the company policy and allow for questions,

4.  to suggest to workers that they avoid the media and help in rumor control.

The human resources director and the union president, armed with accurate information, facilitated this meeting.

## INTERVENTION PROCEDURES

### Preincident Planning

In the case study above, what made for such a successful intervention was planning. The organization had a crisis team that had met prior to the event and had developed a good working relationship. They knew what each team member's responsibilities were. They had negotiated policy and developed strategies to deal with potential problems; so when the incident occurred, they were up and running.

### Needs Assessment

Lets look at how the crisis response team mentioned above assessed needs after the violent incident:

After hearing of the incident team members discussed how to respond. They knew there would be a need for information on the medical condition of the injured party, the legal status of the perpetrator, and the administrative position of the company. With the help of legal counsel, they drafted a memo that covered these points and distributed it to all employees in order to maintain consistency.

Members also understood that the employees who had witnessed the event and tried to intervene would have different issues than those who heard about it third-hand. Within 24 hours, they had informed all employees that there would be a voluntary meeting on company time to discuss the incident.

## Debriefings

A debriefing is a meeting in which individuals affected by a crisis gather with a facilitator to discuss the incident and their reactions to it. Below are the points that differentiate a discussion from a formal debriefing:

A debriefing is a scheduled event.

All members of a designated group are invited.

Usually an outside individual who was not involved in the event (a peer facilitator or someone from the EAP, mental health clinic, or hospital) facilitates the debriefing.

The issues of confidentiality and privacy are addressed specifically.

A debriefing is not a psychotherapy or group counseling session. Participants talk only about the event, not about company politics, personality conflicts, or personnel problems. Although it may be strongly recommended by an organization, attendance is voluntary; participation is encouraged but not demanded of the participants.

A debriefing is a psychoeducational experience that goes through several stages or phases:

1. *Introduction.* The facilitators greet the participants and review the guidelines and structure of the meeting.

2. *Paint the picture.* Each member describes the incident from his or her perspective.

3. *Reactions.* Each member describes his or her reaction at the time of the event or since its occurrence.

4. *Educational.* Facilitators provide information to the participants about the incident, their reactions, and recommendations on how to handle difficult reactions.

5. *Follow up.* The facilitators have some contact with the participants one to two weeks after the debriefing.

The goal of this meeting is to acknowledge that the participants have experienced a traumatic event and to allow them to discuss their reactions as well as receive information and education. Remember:

*prevention = education + communication*

In other words, we can avoid further exacerbation of reactions by offering people education and allowing them to talk openly about their experience.

For more information about conducting debriefings and other interventions, see Lewis, *Critical Incident Stress and Trauma in the Workplace* (1994).

# Chapter 12

# ORGANIZATIONAL HEALTH AND RECOVERY

We have discussed characteristics of individuals and organizations that correlate with hostile and violent acts. Having such information can help an organization ensure a safer workplace: Management can develop policies that prohibit such behaviors and procedures to handle threatening and overtly hostile situations; assess the security of the premises; and evaluate at-risk job applicants and employees. Recognizing that any workplace is vulnerable, an organization can contract with an employee assistance program, mental health professionals, or a mental health agency to provide consultation, evaluations, and debriefings. With such resources in place, managers, supervisors, and employees can be trained to take appropriate actions before, during, and after an incident. But one last preventive action remains: an assessment of the organization's "mental health" and of strategies to correct any deficiencies.

## EMPLOYEE SURVEY

How do we determine an organization's mental health? Ask the people who work there. It is becoming common practice for companies to survey their employees about their satisfaction. An organization should know how workers perceive management, human resources, employee relations, and health services; how they interact with other units and departments and with customers; how they describe their relationships with their supervisors and coworkers; how they feel about wages, benefits, and working conditions; and their overall satisfaction with the employer. Such a survey becomes a benchmark for subsequent annual evaluations and serves to pinpoint those areas needing immediate attention.

There are many competent organizations that design, implement, and analyze employee surveys. Some can even compare your results against those in your industry. Or a company can develop an instrument in-house; however, where mistrust is especially high, the results may be less than honest or useful. An outside vendor brings a professional reputation and can offer protection of each person's confidentiality. In addition, an outsider may successfully arrange focus groups and conduct personal interviews with impunity. Such techniques can provide for more in-depth discussions of employees' views.

Instituting an employee survey by itself begins a healing process because it communicates an employer's interest in its personnel. It says that management is concerned about more than the bottom line. Moreover, if the results are distributed with immediate goals, a plan of action, and a time frame, workers feel acknowledged and supported.

A cautionary note applies here: Where suspicions are overt, employees may remain skeptical and fail to cooperate with a survey, as the case study below demonstrates:

A large newspaper contracted with a consulting firm to survey employee morale. Despite the fact that management gave people time off from their jobs to complete the survey, several of the unions told their memberships to boycott the event. Fortunately, the consulting firm listened to employees' and unions' objection and met with union officials before issuing the survey.

What might an employee survey show? It should examine how employees see management, including their perspectives on official representatives from human resources, employee relations, and health services. These units or departments traditionally carry out decisions made by management, so employee response to the way things operate is often vented on these functionaries. Often, these agents are the recipients of employee wrath as a result of their duties and responsibilities rather than their personalities.

Other people at risk are supervisors. The employee survey allows subordinates to express concerns in a socially acceptable way. Such information educates senior management about how personnel perceive they are being treated. Here is an easy means to identify groups of potentially disgruntled employees and begin taking corrective action.

Since wages, benefits, working conditions, and change often are associated with personnel dissatisfaction, the employee survey also must assess these factors. Together they are referred to as *maintenance functions.* Keep in mind, however, that research has shown that employees are sensitive to the *absence* of these conditions rather than responsive to their presence. Employees see "real changes" as more inside information, more responsibility over their work, and more input into decision-making.

## THE FIVE *As* OF ORGANIZATIONAL HEALTH

Figure 12.1 shows the five specific features of organizational health, as discussed by Lewis (1994). They are attitude, awareness, acknowledgment, availability, and appreciation.

> *Attitude:* A company's attitude should be positive, honest, and open. Employees want to hear that management has set goals and is headed in a positive direction. They expect honest information about the status of the business, even if the news is grim. More and more organizations are teaching their workers how to read financial reports and to see how their efforts contribute to the bottom line. Such open

communication gives employees easy access to both information and management. They become partners in the enterprise.

*Awareness:* Awareness of employees' reactions is another factor in organizational health. As management listens and observes what its workers are saying and doing, it gains insight into how to improve productivity and team work. Companies that encourage their employees to state their views and become part of the process benefit from increased loyalty, higher levels of output, and greater profits. Being aware of what employees think, perceive, and feel enhances management's ability to steer the organization.

*Acknowledgment:* A mentally healthy company acknowledges reality. Whatever the issue may be—the cost of supplies, the level of sales, new technology, or possibilities of a hostile takeover—management tells employees exactly what is happening, without sugar-coating the news or denying its impact. Employees are notified well in advance of any changes. Often they are included in decision making, implementation, and evaluation processes. The organization recognizes important changes by giving workers time to discuss issues, air their feelings, and understand options.

---

1. **A**ttitude is positive, honest, and open
2. **A**wareness of employee reactions
3. **A**cknowledgment of transition and reactions
4. **A**vailability of management
5. **A**ppreciation of all employees' efforts

**Figure 12.1.** The five *A*s of organizational health.

*Availability:* Organizational health means that managers are available. When stress rises, supervisors have a tendency to hide behind closed doors. Naturally, the amount of work is high, justifying such behavior. But by insulating themselves from workers, they lose access to information about working conditions, morale, and personal events. As one individual quipped, "It's not just managing by walking around; it's managing by stopping to talk with employees."

The psychological distance between management and labor is bridged when people see and talk to each other at the workplace. Employees have a better chance of communicating their concerns when they are in close proximity to management. Simultaneously, management's awareness of potential pitfalls grows, so that potential problems are identified early.

*Appreciation:* People hunger for acknowledgment of their contributions, and management must show its appreciation of employee efforts. Especially during rough times, workers must hear kind words and receive a pat on the back. A healthy organization is a humane one. Sadly, humane workplaces are rare, although they should be the norm. Developing a humane workplace requires a strong, steady vision of what it looks and feels like and the belief that any and all work units can recover from dysfunction. The enormous costs of a toxic atmosphere should provide enough motivation for directors, supervisors, and line staff to transform unhealthy workplaces into productive, profitable, and nurturing environments.

## THE HUMANE WORKPLACE

Imagine the joy of waking up and being eager to go to work. Your relationships with your coworkers provide both satisfaction and stimulation. Mutual respect presides. Everyone seems dedicated and committed to and responsible for serving customers efficiently and effectively. Individual growth and creativity blossom within a hothouse of productivity. Work is fun as people collaborate in solving problems and getting things done.

Humane organizations value the collective good and individuality. They allow self-determination, dignity, and respect while optimizing the use of individual and natural resources. They use each person's unique talents, gifts, energies, and efforts and acknowledge the contributions of all participants through formal award systems and informal expressions of appreciation. When employees are happy and content, an organization reaps the benefits through customer satisfaction, financial stability, and unexcelled reputation.

No one wants to work in an unhealthy situation. Yet humane worksites are few and far between. How ironic that human services workers who care passionately about their clients often find themselves working for organizations in which they are mistreated and even abused. As individuals and as employers, we can ill afford the consequences of less-than-ideal working conditions.

People who work in toxic environments are at greater risk for health problems, depression, and addictive behaviors. They are more apt to become ill, be injured on the job, make mistakes, work inefficiently, mistreat coworkers and customers, behave in hostile or even violent ways, and eventually leave their jobs prematurely. Such actions translate into higher costs of doing business because of absenteeism, workers' compensation claims, lowered productivity, customer complaints, and turnover. This invisible drain of dollars inflates the budgets of most human services organizations.

## MANAGEMENT–LABOR RELATIONS

In chapter 4, we discussed theory X management—a system that fosters mutual distrust and disrespect between management and labor. The case studies that follow demonstrate two examples of workplace toxicity, and Dr. Zare's efforts to develop human working environments.

## Case Study #1

Between 1987 and 1994, I was the director of an internal and external employee assistance program based in a community hospital. Along with two other programs, the EAP reported to the outpatient substance abuse department, which had a history of problems dating back 20 years. Among the problems were frequent staff turnover, low productivity and morale, and periodic conflicts between managers and line workers.

Gossip dominated worker interactions, as people openly expressed their distrust of management. One program after another was identified as dysfunctional. Employees within the "problem program" claimed that its manager was treating them unfairly. This charge was leveled at each program manager and then the department head in turn until a key person within the unit resigned, usually within a 6- to 18- month period. At that point, the issue would subside and another program and its administrator would occupy center stage. Honeymoon periods with new employees were short-lived and always followed by covert hostility.

Within a few weeks of becoming the director, I became a target for employee hostility. It seemed the problem was solved when one of the program staff resigned two months later. However, the true nature of the situation resurfaced when her replacement joined the unit and the pattern was repeated. Now the division between line staff and management became apparent. Whatever each party said or did was scrutinized unmercifully, usually to the other side's detriment. Staff meetings were particularly painful because of the deafening silences and loud accusations. Both management and labor felt disrespected, devalued, and abused.

It might seem that, as the boss, I held the advantage. After all, I could assign people unpleasant tasks, large workloads, and difficult schedules, or manipulate the work in a dissatisfying way. Furthermore, as manager, I conducted perfor-

mance evaluations and so could make periodic public judgments that were entered onto employee records. Yet line
workers also have considerable power over their manager
in how they do the job. To a large degree, they control the
delivery of services and could make or break the program's
reputation (and mine). Since both sides contributed to the
overall atmosphere, we each suffered as we trudged into
the office every day, wishing we were elsewhere. What
could I do?

The key to unlocking this puzzle was holding a strong, clear
vision of what our program could look like and be in the
future. Fortunately, I had such a vision, the determination
to make it materialize, and the support of the department
head to implement it. The line workers embraced my vision, although neither side knew how to make it happen
under the circumstances. Yet we had taken our first step
toward recovery in being united by our common mission.
However, staff doubted I could accomplish it because the
hospital administration had never done such things before.
I persevered, with the result that small changes occurred.
As I kept the vision before us, the tensions began to dis-
solve. My credibility increased. Staff wanted to be part of
this emerging, successful program rather than continue the
dysfunctional pattern.

While I cannot say the vision alone turned the tide, I know
it was a major component. The vision articulated a description and operation of a humane workplace. I saw an office
where staff enjoyed coming to work and engaging with
each other, where people exercised initiative and took responsibility for solving customer problems, where customers received the highest quality of services for a reasonable
price, where I and other staff were leaders in the EAP field
throughout our service area.

I began to behave at work as if these objectives had already
been met. I regularly praised employees, finding examples
of their devotion and effort in getting the job done. More-

over, I asked each line staff member about his or her long-term career goals and I supported these goals by assigning work and scheduling conference times in concert with them. I negotiated for up-to-date equipment and pleasant office space. I organized impromptu parties. Despite the fact that salaries were frozen, we discovered ways to reward productivity other than through wages by giving time off and offering flexible work schedules.

The results were outstanding. Turnover dropped to zero. Other employees within the department, as well as outside applicants, flocked to new job openings. Our program grew from 3 to 12 members, plus 20 fee-for-service consultants; from serving 2,500 households to more than 20,000; from serving 8 organizations to working with more than 50; from grossing $100,000 to more than $500,000. Perhaps the best indicator was being unable to distinguish between work and fun.

## Case Study #2

The second example comes from a different perspective. In this situation, I was a line worker. Within weeks of accepting the position, I saw and felt the dysfunction. Gossip abounded. The major topic was how poorly administration treated workers. Every memo, casual encounter, and staff meeting was grist for the mill. As a newcomer, other employees were eager to orient me to the situation, to tell me their side of the tale.

I observed the division between workers when we came together at staff meetings: blacks supported blacks; support staff stood against professional workers; and line staff squared off against management. The other symptom I noted was that some of my colleagues had resigned themselves to doing their jobs without any emotional input. They seemed like the patients on antipsychotic medication who shuffle back and forth in the day rooms of psychiatric wards with little affect, purpose, or understanding.

Knowing how a humane workplace operates, I was determined to bring this vision and experience to my agency. Since I was not in a designated leadership position, I couldn't impose these views on my coworkers; yet I could act on them. Guided by the vision, I deliberately said "Hello" each morning to administrators, support staff, and professional workers. I praised accomplishments in private and at staff meetings and complimented people on results. Seeking to bridge the gap between support staff and professional workers, I organized a potluck luncheon to mark secretary's day. I celebrated special occasions like birthdays and holidays with cards, food, or inexpensive gifts. Moreover, I openly shared my vision of a humane workplace.

The results were gratifying. People's attitudes changed. There were smiles, camaraderie, and eagerness to engage in group activities. While I'm unaware of the financial impact, the number of customers served steadily increased while the staffing levels remained constant. I can only assume that revenues went up. Most important, I and other staff felt better about coming to work and had a heightened commitment to the job.

## PRINCIPLES OF TRANSFORMATION

At what point does a work organization become toxic? This question has no clear answer and depends on many variables. However, once sickened by the disease process, the organization must make recovery its first priority. Otherwise, the illness quickly invades every facet of the agency's work and could lead to its downfall or even to hostile and violent behavior on the part of employees.

As in a 12-step program, *acceptance* is the first step in changing circumstances. Unless people acknowledge the frustration, disappointment, and unhappiness within the agency, employees cannot focus their energies on making things better. Instead they are consumed by gossip and acting out the victim's role. A catalyst is needed to proclaim that the workplace is suffering. Only then can an organized effort begin to examine and change the environment. Unfortunately, all too often the catalyst is an incident of overt hostility or violence. At that point the company often reacts to the incident rather than responding to the problem.

At this point leaders must step forward to paint a vivid picture of what a healthy organization looks like to inspire motivation and concentrate energies in the right direction. Having a vision of what the organization could be shapes the intervention. How can we best deliver services to our customers? How can we interact with each other to maximize communication, respect, and rapport? Many CEOs do this in large meetings and only once. It is essential that employees see and have access to and contact with as many key decision makers as possible as often as possible.

At times of crisis, the workplace family needs contact, reassurance, and guidance. Key people must also understand that the anxiety and apprehension in the workplace is a normal reaction. Morale may fluctuate and must be supported through kind words and gracious deeds. People hunger for acknowledgment and encouragement and drink in praise like a cactus stores moisture. Rather than note extraordinary work, leaders should compliment the simple and mundane, as long as the individual is performing well and completing his or her tasks. Leadership must have patience and compassion and view employees much as a coach would approach a team training for the Olympics—its a long course, with ups and downs. The team must pace itself, receive nurturing along the way, and give and receive lots of encouragement.

Employees must also understand that management is facing a new course. The changes affecting the American workplace are unique and call for new strategies and interventions. Patience and understanding on the part of employees at all levels are essential.

There is never enough communication at times of transition. Whether in a family or in a workplace, communication is the key to establishing trust. Most organizations practice the age-old art of *talking to employees* rather than *talking with them.* We are often asked to train people to manage change in the workplace. Usually the request is inspired by upper or middle management in a credible effort to provide relief to the organization. The belief is that having someone from outside come in and lecture on the reactions to change will somehow change those reactions. Often the groups are divided between management and nonmanagement, as if there is a different message for each.

The preferred model for such a training program is a mixed group from all layers within the organization. First, we provide them with a facilitative format through which they can communicate with each other about their concerns. Second, we focus on strategies to help in the transition process. Having only one program for managing change is of little value to an organization. It is like going to the gym for one workout. Since transition is an ongoing process, ample time must be spent focusing the energies of the organization on that process. Many organizations are in a state of denial over the impact of change on the workforce. We often hear from upper management, "We are spending too much time talking about the changes and not enough time doing them." At times of transition, there can never be too much communication. It is the antidote to the toxicity that develops as an organization deals with change.

As the process continues the organization must spend time celebrating its successes. The group needs to enjoy its victories. By coming together and marking its progress, people develop a sense of camaraderie and build teamwork. Now the change effort becomes self-sustaining.

Certainly attention must be focused on hostility and violence in the workplace and how to respond to it. Yet, this may closing the barn door after the horse is out. Organizations are often penny-wise and pound-foolish when it come to spending money on preventative programs. Establishing a humane workplace requires leadership at all levels and people who can identify the problem, hold and share the vision, boost morale, and acknowledge and celebrate success.

When these steps are applied *consistently over time*, the toxic workplace may be transformed into a safe and productive environment.

## SUMMARY

As the world and the workplace move toward the 21st century, we are increasingly aware of the changes facing individuals, families, communities, countries, and the workplace. Change produces stress, and stress produces reactions. The majority of people cope quite well with the stresses of life; however, there is a growing risk pool of people who become overwhelmed and develop maladaptive reactions. Drugs, alcohol, marital, familial, financial, emotional, and physical impairments develop if people cannot manage the stresses of their lives.

Currently, there is great concern about violence in our society and in the workplace. Certainly, we should make every effort to respond whenever possible. However, we must do so in an effective and proactive manner that does not escalate the issue with hype and hysteria. The workplace is actually safer than it has been at any other time in recorded history. In the last 50 years, new laws and policies have improved the quality, comfort, and safety of most workplaces.

While there is a great deal of concern about the disgruntled worker—the one who might go off at any moment—the majority of workplace hostility and violence is not perpetrated by employees or former employees. In fact, most homicides in the workplace occur as a result of robberies by strangers. Further, nonfatal assaults are committed mainly by patients or others within the healthcare system, not by employees. Myths abound when it comes to workplace hostility and violence. Most are ill-founded.

Internally generated hostility and violence usually are caused by stress and toxicity that develop within the organization. Like an infection, they may spread and damage the entire organization if left untreated—sometimes erupting in overt acts of violence by at-risk employees. More often, hostility is subtle, less well delineated, and distributed throughout the organization in less intense but nonetheless damaging forms of behavior.

We had several aims in writing this book:

to provide an objective and realistic overview of workplace hostility;

to differentiate and define different types of hostile behavior;

to provide clear guidelines for assessing at-risk individuals;

to define at-risk and toxic workplaces;

to provide guidelines for organizations to manage hostility from within and from outside of the workplace;

to describe the role of the EA profession; and, finally,

to describe the healthy organization and how to become one.

Books may been written, assessments completed, policies developed, training programs given. But to combat hostility and violence in the workplace, we must first work to establish and maintain a culture of *trust*. Only through trust will respect and responsibility prevail and hostility and violence diminish Trust takes:

|  |  |
|---|---|
| **T** | time and tolerance |
| **R** | respect and responsibility |
| **U** | unity and understanding |
| **S** | safety and structure |
| **T** | thoughtfulness and thanks |

# Bibliography

Baron, R. A., & Neuman, J. H. (1995). Workplace violence and workplace aggression: Evidence on their relative frequency and potential causes. *Aggressive Behavior, 22,* 161–173.

Barrier, M. (1995). The enemy within. *Nation's Business, 83,* 18–24.

Bates, N. D., & Donnell, S. (1993). *Major developments in premises security liability.* Sudbury, MA: Liability Consultants, Inc.

Bridges, W. (1991). *Managing transitions.* Reading, MA: Addison-Wesley.

Casstillo, D. N., & Jenkins, E. L. (1994). Industries and occupations at high risk for work-related homicide. *Journal of Occupational Medicine, 36*(2): 125–132.

Cembrowics, S. P., & Shepard, J. P. (1992). Violence in the accident and emergency department. *Medical Science Law, 32*(2): 118–122.

Centers for Disease Control (CDC). Occupational injury and deaths—United States, 1980-89. *Morbidity and Mortality Weekly Report, 43*(32), 587, 593-595.

Department of Transportation (DOT). (1994). *1994 motor vehicle crash data report.* Washington, DC: U.S. Government Printing Office.

DiLorenzo, L., & Carroll, D. (1995, March). Screening applicants for a safer workplace. *HR Magazine, 40,* 55–56.

Federal Bureau of Investigation (FBI). (1995). *Uniform crime report: Crime in the U.S, 1994.* Washington, DC: U.S. Department of Justice.

Gerson, A. (1993). A violent state of mind? *Occupational Health & Safety, 62,* 64–67.

Gilligan, J. (1996). *Violence: Our deadly epidemic and its causes.* New York: Grosset/Putnam.

Hughes, T. (1995, August 7). Workplace violence programs can help minimize an employer's risk. *Massachusetts Lawyers Weekly,* 1–2.

Kenney, J. (1995). *Breaking point: The workplace violence epidemic and what to do about it.* Charlotte, NC: National Safe Workplace Institute.

Labig, C. E. (1995a). *Preventing violence in the workplace.* New York: AMACOM.

Labig, C. E. (1995b, August). Workplace security: Forming a violence response team. *HR Focus, 72,* 15–16.

Landry, J. T. (1997). Workplace violence: Preventing the unthinkable. *Harvard Business Review, 75,* 11–12.

Lewis, G. (1993). Managing crises and trauma in the workplace: How to respond and intervene. *AAOHN Journal, 41*(3), 124–130.

Lewis, G. (1994). *Critical incident stress and trauma in the workplace.* Muncie, IN: Accelerated Development.

McCune, J. C. (1994, March). Companies grapple with workplace violence. *Management Review, 83,* 52-57.

Mantell, M., with S. Albrecht. (1994). *Ticking bombs: Defusing violence in the workplace.* Burr Ridge, IL: Irwin Professional Publishers.

National Institute on Drug Abuse. (1997). *National household survey on drug abuse: Main findings, 1995.* Rockville, MD: U.S. Department of Public Health Services.

National Institute for Occupational Safety and Health (NIOSH). (1996a, June). *Current intelligence bulletin.* Washington, DC: Government Printing Office.

National Institute for Occupational Safety and Health (NIOSH). (1996b). *Violence in the workplace: Risk factors and prevention strategies.* Washington, DC: Government Printing Office.

Neergaard, L. (1993). "Depression's annual cost pegged at $43.7 billion." *Boston Globe* (December 1).

Nigro, L. G., & Waugh, W. L. (1996). Violence in the American workplace: Challenges to the public employer. *Public Administration Review, 56*(4), 326–333.

Noer, D. (1993). *Healing the wounds.* San Francisco: Jossey-Bass.

Noer, D. (1997). *Breaking free.* San Francisco: Jossey-Bass.

Nova Scotia Occupational Health and Safety Advisory Council. (1995). *Protection of workers from violence in the workplace.* Halifax, Nova Scotia. Information available from: Legislation for Policy Review, P.O. Box 697, Halifax, Nova Scotia B3J 2T8.

Pastor, L. H. (1995). Initial assessment and intervention strategies to reduce workplace violence. *American Family Physician, 52*(4), 1169–1175.

Ryan, K., & Oestreich, D. (1991). *Driving fear out of the workplace.* San Francisco: Jossey-Bass.

Smith, W. H. (1995, April 22–23). *Violence in the workplace: A family systems perspective. The emotional side of organizations: Applications of Bowen theory.* Washington, DC: Papers presented at Georgetown Family Center's Conference on Organizations.

Steinhauer, J. (1997, March 27). If the boss is out of line, what's the legal boundary? *New York Times,* D1, D4.

Tarlow, D. (1995, August 7). The duty to protect employees from violent acts. *Massachusetts Lawyers Weekly.*

U.S. Department of Health and Human Services; Public Health Service; Alcohol, Drug Abuse, Mental Health Administrator. (Jan. 1990). *Seventh Special Report to U.S. Congress on Alcohol and Health.* Rockville, MD: Author.

U.S. Department of Justice, Office of Justice Programs. (1996). *Criminal victimization, 1996.* Washington, DC: Author.

Weber, M. (1947) *The theory of social and economic organization.* Glencoe, IL: Free Press.

Williams, A. H. (1997). Workplace violence: 10 steps to a safer workplace. *HR Focus, 74,* 9–10.

Wortham, S. (1996). Violence rips through the global workplace. *Safety & Health, 154,* 46–49.

# Index

# About the Authors

**Gerald Lewis, Ph.D.,** is a clinical psychologist who has practiced in the Boston area for 20 years. He was chief psychologist at the Marlboro Hospital and remains on its medical staff. He received his doctorate degree from the George Washington University in 1977.

In 1985, Dr. Lewis went into private practice and, as codirector, he organized Mental Health Affiliates of Marlboro and

Framingham, a multidisciplinary group of mental health professionals.

In 1986, in an effort to combine his clinical experience with his training and consultation skills, he founded COMPASS—Comprehensive Assessment and Consultation. COMPASS provides employee assistance programs, consultation, and training services.

Dr. Lewis has addressed businesses, treatment agencies, schools, and professional organizations around the world on a wide variety of mental health, work, and family issues. His first book, *Critical Incident Stress and Trauma in the Workplace*, was published in 1994.

He is the assistant team coordinator of the MASSPORT (Logan Airport) CISD Team. He has conducted training for the U.S. Postal Service, the U.S. Army, the Office for Personnel Management, federal occupational health services, and the Federal Aviation Association. He also has provided training for the Bank of Montreal and the Panama Canal Commission.

**Nancy Zare, D.S.W.,** associate professor in the School of Human Services at Springfield College in Springfield, Massachusetts, founded EnvisioNZ, a consulting organization dedicated to promoting effective communication in the workplace. She is an authority on substance abuse and holds a master's degree and doctorate in social planning from Boston College.

A professional member of the National Speakers Association, Dr. Zare frequently presents workshops on succeeding with difficult people, making the most of change, and before violence comes to work. She is known for her ability to condense complex ideas into simple, practical information, enabling her clients to understand differences and adopt winning strategies, relieve individual and organizational stress, and establish workplaces that respect both people and profits.

Dr. Zare lives in Framingham, Massachusetts, and is an avid gardener and swimmer.